THE
BEATLE
BANDIT

THE BEATLE BANDIT

A SERIAL BANK ROBBER'S DEADLY HEIST,
A CROSS-COUNTRY MANHUNT, AND THE
INSANITY PLEA THAT SHOOK THE NATION

NATE HENDLEY

DUNDURN
PRESS

Publisher and acquiring editor: Scott Fraser | Editor: Laurie Miller
Cover designer: Laura Boyle
Cover image: © Government of Canada. Reproduced with the permission of Library and Archives Canada (2021). Source: Library and Archives Canada/Department of Justice fonds/C-0149611.
Printer: Marquis Book Printing Inc.

Library and Archives Canada Cataloguing in Publication

Title: The Beatle Bandit : a serial bank robber's deadly heist, a cross-country manhunt, and the insanity plea that shook the nation / Nate Hendley.
Names: Hendley, Nate, author.
Description: Includes bibliographical references and index.
Identifiers: Canadiana (print) 20210260564 | Canadiana (ebook) 20210260572 |
 ISBN 9781459748101 (softcover) | ISBN 9781459748118 (PDF) | ISBN 9781459748125 (EPUB)
Subjects: LCSH: Smith, Matthew Kerry. | LCSH: Bank robberies—Ontario—Toronto. | LCSH: Murder—Ontario—Toronto.
Classification: LCC HV6665.C32 H46 2021 | DDC 364.15/5209713541—dc23

We acknowledge the support of the Canada Council for the Arts and the Ontario Arts Council for our publishing program. We also acknowledge the financial support of the Government of Ontario, through the Ontario Book Publishing Tax Credit and Ontario Creates, and the Government of Canada.

Dundurn Press
1382 Queen Street East
Toronto, Ontario, Canada M4L 1C9
dundurn.com, @dundurnpress 𝕐 f ⓞ

This book is dedicated to Paul Truster, who first alerted me to the story of Matthew Kerry Smith and provided interview contacts and copious research materials. This book would not have been possible without Paul's dedication and commendable research skills.

Contents

Introduction

This book is about Matthew Kerry Smith, who robbed a series of banks in Southern Ontario between 1960 and 1964 — most notably, the Canadian Imperial Bank of Commerce in North York on July 24, 1964. On this occasion, Smith shot and killed a bank customer named Jack Blanc who tried to intervene.

Smith's actions would have far-reaching effects and inflame a national debate about gun control, the insanity defence, and especially, the death penalty in Canada.

His crimes were particularly shocking given that Canada prided itself on being a peaceful society at the time with a low crime rate. Gunfights on the street with military-grade weapons happened in Chicago, not Canada.

The 1961 census counted 18.24 million Canadians. Of these, 1.8 million people lived in the Metropolitan Toronto Area, making it the second-largest urban centre in the country, after Montreal.

Metro Toronto was not a particularly diverse place. Over a million residents responding to the 1961 census cited the "British Isles" as their homeland. Most of the remaining residents in Metropolitan Toronto came from continental Europe. Protestants represented the majority faith in Metro Toronto, and there were few people of colour (although the 1961 census did list 20,534 residents under the category "Asiatic"). At the time, North York was an independent municipality with a population of 269,959 and its own mayor.

In the summer of 1964, Philip Givens was mayor of Toronto. He presided over a rapidly growing city that had to deal with multiple issues. The day Smith conducted his raid on the Imperial Bank, the *Toronto Daily Star* reported on a meeting of municipal officials "to discuss a proposed apartment development with local homeowners."

The meeting quickly degenerated into "a general beefing session against the city," reported the *Star*. Homeowners raised angry questions about taxes, the high cost of snow removal, and noise from subway construction, among other topics.

Then, as now, Toronto was considered a safe place. Even in 2020 there were only seventy-one homicides in the City of Toronto, down from seventy-nine the year before, a remarkably low figure for a "mega-city" where nearly three million people currently live.

In the 1960s, violent crime was even less common. Toronto had its share of headline-grabbing criminals, such as the bank-robbing Boyd Gang of the early 1950s, but the city was generally peaceful. So, too, was the entire country, for that matter.

In 1964, there were 253 homicides recorded in Canada, 81 of which took place in Ontario. That same year, Canadian courts handed down five death sentences. While no one had been executed since late 1962, when Ronald Turpin and Arthur Lucas were hanged at Toronto's Don Jail, capital punishment was still on the books.

If Canadian crime rates were low, violence and armed robbery were not completely unknown.

On July 24, 1964, the front page of the *Toronto Daily Star* carried a story about a bank robbery in small-town Cobden, Ontario. During a holdup at a Bank of Nova Scotia branch, a pair of robbers shot and wounded a bank accountant. A teller was held hostage and two suspects were arrested in a stolen vehicle at the west gate of Algonquin Park.

The same edition offered a glimpse at the entertainment options available to Torontonians in the summer of 1964. There were advertisements for an upcoming Louis Armstrong concert and the musical *Camelot*. A small notice listed a show by then-unknown Levon Helm (before his fame with the Band). The big movies in town included *Robin and the 7 Hoods* (a clownish affair featuring Frank Sinatra's Rat Pack), Stanley Kubrick's *Dr. Strangelove*, and *Zulu*, featuring an up-and-coming British actor named Michael Caine.

As for more downscale entertainment, a Toronto theatre offered an adults-only flick called *The Doctor and the Playgirls*, supposedly based on the "Profumo-Keeler-Dr. Ward Scandal!" as the ad copy put it. Said scandal involved sex, prostitutes, and British high society. The same theatre promised a demonstration of "the latest in beach fashions including the new and unique topless bathing suits, modeled by the world's most beautiful women."

On a similar note, Toronto's Victory Burlesque theatre was hosting a performance by Kim Soo Lee, "sexotic Queen of the Orient!" An advertisement assured attendees they could enjoy a "great stage and screen show in cool air-conditioned comfort."

During the summer of 1964, Toronto residents could look forward to exciting hockey action once the new season commenced. That spring, the Toronto Maple Leafs had stomped the Detroit Red Wings 4–0 in the seventh game of the finals, to win their third consecutive Stanley Cup. The Leafs were helmed by legendary coach George "Punch" Imlach and featured stars such as Frank Mahovlich, Johnny Bower, and Tim Horton (whose name is now associated with the nationwide doughnut and coffee chain he co-founded). Anyone who followed hockey in 1964 could be forgiven for assuming the Leafs were unbeatable.

South of the border, the United States was convulsed by the civil rights movement and growing unrest in African American communities. The July 24, 1964, edition of the *Star* contained the headline "Barry, Johnson to Meet on Civil Rights" (referencing pro–civil rights president Lyndon Johnson and Republican party nominee Barry Goldwater). The same page featured a photograph of a "young Negro" as the cutline called him, arrested for suspected vandalism in Brooklyn.

In Canada, things were considerably more mundane. Lester Pearson was prime minister, and the Liberal Party ran the government. The big issue of the day was "Should Canada have a new flag?" and if yes, "What should it look like?"

In 1964, Canada waved an emblem featuring a modified Union Jack called the Canadian Red Ensign. Rancorous debate about the state of Canada's flag kicked off in the House of Commons in June 1964. The new flag, featuring a red maple leaf against a white background, bracketed by red bars, would be unveiled in early 1965.

The other earth-shattering news in Canada in 1964 was the arrival of a musical quartet from Liverpool called the Beatles. Like most western nations at the time, Canada was swept up in "Beatlemania" as the Fab Four repeatedly topped the charts. Toronto teens dreamed about seeing the Beatles perform live at a pair of shows scheduled for the Maple Leaf Gardens hockey arena that September. The Beatles would return to perform in Toronto in 1965 and 1966, but their initial appearances sparked by far the largest frenzy.

Big Toronto radio stations such as CHUM and CKEY kept watch over this mayhem, encouraging it at times. The stations were rivals and tried to outdo each other with wild promotional stunts. The CKEY crew referred to themselves as the "Good Guys."

Matthew Kerry Smith would take note of the impacts of both the Beatles and radio station CKEY during his violent robbery of the Imperial Bank.

This crime would have national repercussions and be a personal tragedy for Smith's victims and his family alike.

Note: Most of the events in this book occurred before Canada converted to the metric system. Media articles and official documentation cited use imperial measurements (pounds, feet, yards, etc.). To avoid confusion, I have primarily used imperial measurements throughout the text to present a consistent narrative.

Note Two: There are no "imagined" conversations in this book. All comments, conversations, and dialogue are based on court transcripts, interviews, newspaper articles, police documents, etc. In general, quotes from interviews are in present tense while quotes from other sources are in past tense. All sources are cited in the bibliography.

Chapter One

Bullets, Banks, and Beatle Wigs

On the afternoon of July 24, 1964, Matthew Kerry Smith drove to the intersection of North York's Overbrook Place and Elder Street in a modified Ford Galaxie that contained guns, a wig, and a guitar case, among other items. He parked and began to prepare for the armed robbery he'd been planning. It was Friday, and the weather was sunny and hot. Smith's target — the Canadian Imperial Bank of Commerce at nearby Bathurst Manor Plaza — was dealing with the last customers of the day.

The intelligent but troubled son of a successful businessman and mentally ill mother, twenty-four-year-old Smith had more than just money on his mind. He harboured dreams of a revolution and viewed bank robbery as a means of financing it.

Smith had previously robbed two other banks at gunpoint and seized thousands of dollars. He had tried and failed to steal weapons from an armoury and been jailed for leading police on a wild car chase. Prior to these criminal exploits, Smith served in the Royal Canadian Navy (RCN).

Still in his car, Smith was clad in a white T-shirt bearing the slogan "CKEY Good Guys," referring to the local radio station. He ducked beneath the dashboard and put on his disguise, which consisted of a Halloween mask depicting the face of French president Charles de Gaulle, sunglasses, and a long-haired Beatle wig. The Fab Four from England were all the rage, and Toronto retailers had started selling wigs modelled after the band's shaggy locks. A few months earlier, Harold Ballard, president of Maple Leaf Gardens, had donned one of these wigs to greet fans lined up to buy tickets for that first pair of Beatles concerts.

On March 23, 1964, the Beatles had six songs in CKEY-rival CHUM's hit parade top ten, although the day of the Canadian Imperial Bank of Commerce (CIBC) robbery the number one song at CHUM was "Memphis" by Johnny Rivers — a brief hiatus from the Beatles' onslaught.

Smith was heavily armed. His main weapon of choice was an air-cooled, gas-powered Fabrique Nationale (FN) .308 (7.62 mm) semi-automatic rifle. For backup, Smith packed a .45-caliber semi-automatic pistol in a belt holster.

Dubbed "the quintessential battle rifle," the long, lethal FN was developed in Belgium and used by soldiers around the world. The Canadian Army was equipped with a licensed, made-in-Ontario version of the FN rifle called the C-1.

It was the type of firearm to give you pause — even if Smith had painted the barrel of his weapon pink. The rest of his rifle was black. There was some logic behind Smith's choice of colour. He intended to approach the bank on foot, hiding his rifle in a guitar case. Unfortunately, the rifle was longer than the guitar case. So, prior to the heist, Smith had drilled a hole in one end of the guitar case large enough for the rifle barrel. Smith now placed the FN rifle inside the case, carefully poking the pink barrel through the hole. He snapped the guitar case shut and exited his car.

Anyone who glanced his way would see a guitar case with a pink, metallic object sticking out of it and never guess it was part of a rifle.

Smith got out of the Ford Galaxie, holding his guitar case and a pair of canvas haversacks. In his odd attire, he walked the short distance to the bank. Bathurst Manor Plaza was on Wilmington Avenue, which ran north/south. The CIBC branch was at 221 Wilmington, next to Overbrook, which ran east/west. Also called the Wilmington Plaza, the shopping centre consisted of a nondescript cluster of retail and service outlets facing a parking lot.

A few people on the street gaped as the tall, lanky young man passed by. To make it look like he was a harmless goofball, Smith affected a causal bantering manner, calling out, "Hi, cats!" to a group of young people hanging around the parking lot.

Guitar case in hand, Smith walked through the parking lot and toward the CIBC branch. The bank had a vestibule and double doors. An exterior sign above an awning announced the presence of the CANADIAN IMPERIAL BANK OF COMMERCE in bold capital letters. Big windows along the south wall offered a view of the outside.

Inside the bank, twenty-four-year-old accountant Carman Lamb was fetching American currency for a customer. He looked out the window and saw Smith heading toward the bank. Taking note of the stranger's appearance, Lamb turned to a colleague and joshed, "There goes your brother!"

Lamb went back to his tasks as Smith stepped inside. It was roughly 5:05 p.m.

Smith's attire instantly drew the attention of the roughly two dozen customers in the bank. Some thought he was pulling a prank. Sally Blanc, who was in the bank with her husband, Jack, would later tell a courtroom that Smith "looked like a clown."

At fifty-four years old, Jack Blanc was short and muscular, with dark hair, a moustache, and a soldierly bearing. He worked as a furrier — a maker of fur garments — and was a veteran of both the Canadian Army and the Haganah (a predecessor of the Israel Defense Forces).

Jack and Sally Blanc had two children: daughter Diane, in her midtwenties, and son Stanley, fourteen, who went by the nickname "Butch." The Blanc family — save for Diane, who resided elsewhere — lived in an apartment building at 242 Wilmington Avenue. Their unit overlooked Bathurst Manor Plaza. That Sunday, the family was intending to go on vacation.

"My husband and I went in to open a joint bank account for our holidays, so that we would know exactly how much money we were spending and there wouldn't be any complications financially. We were both quite happy. We were going on a holiday to the States with our son," Sally Blanc later recounted on an episode of the CBC-TV program *Toronto File.*

"We were supposed to go to Kingston first, because I wanted to see Fort Henry and then go back to Windsor, and go to Detroit, to see my father's younger brother," recalls Stanley today.

Some bank customers recognized the CKEY name on Smith's T-shirt and wondered if he was taking part in a publicity stunt. These thoughts ended when Smith opened the guitar case and took out the FN rifle with the pink barrel. He held the rifle in his right hand with the stock resting on his hip, the pair of canvas haversacks in his left hand.

Smith stepped to the northwest corner of the bank, to the office of manager Henry Martens. Martens was inside chatting with salesman Hartley Lepofsky when Smith kicked the door open. The men looked up in surprise at this outlandish character in the doorway. Martens noticed the barrel of the weapon pointed at him was pink and briefly wondered if it was a toy gun.

"He was dressed in cartoon fashion, like a comedian of some sort … He ordered us behind the cages, which I did not understand what he meant. He followed with another instruction to move, and we both just sat there looking at him thinking it was a practical joke or something at the beginning," Lepofsky later testified.

What Smith had to say, however, was anything but funny.

"This is a holdup! I want all the money!" shouted Smith.

Martens didn't react right away.

"I don't think this is very funny," huffed the bank manager.

To show he meant business, Smith fired a shot a few feet above Martens' head. The bullet blasted a hole in the wall measuring one inch in diameter and one-a-half-inches deep.

"When I saw the hole in the wall, I knew this could be no joke, and the noise itself had brought me back to reality," stated Lepofsky.

At the front of the bank, Lamb was stunned by the sound.

"I don't know if you've ever heard a .308 in a close space," he says today. Patrons and staff alike froze in place.

"Get moving! I mean business!" snarled Smith, behind the mask and shades.

With the FN rifle pointed at them, Martens and Lepofsky scurried out of the office. They headed behind the bank counters as staff and customers milled about in shock. Lamb also noticed that the barrel of Smith's weapon was painted pink.

The rifle "was metal rather than nice wood stock [and] about four inches of pink barrel were sticking out of the end. I'm sure I thought 'that's different' but I wasn't giving it that much thought because we're in the middle of a holdup," recalls the accountant.

Witnesses also took note of Smith's headgear. Even people who might not otherwise be fans recognized the Beatle wig. The Beatles were everywhere that year, their pudding-bowl haircuts an endless source of media fascination.

Smith tossed the canvas haversacks over the bank counter. Then, he pressed his left palm against the smooth surface of the counter and leapt over it, tucking his FN rifle under his right arm and hip as he vaulted.

Smith stood on top of Lamb's desk and shouted, "This is a holdup!" For good measure, he added, "Hurry up, because robbing banks is a tough way to make a living."

People weren't sure how to take these remarks. Was the robber trying to be funny or issuing a threat? Regardless of his motivation, everyone tried to stay calm. According to Lamb, everything was "dead quiet" inside the bank. One staffer did have the presence of mind to activate the silent alarm, alerting police that a holdup was in progress.

Smith ordered the tellers to empty their tills and place the cash in his haversack bags. Martens instructed the tellers to do as they were told, and hand over the money from their tills. As tellers stuffed cash inside the bags, Smith said, "I'm not satisfied with the till money. I want all you have."

This meant accessing the vault and the money inside. Opening the bank vault, however, required the actions of three people: Martens, accountant Lamb, and first teller Joan Hoffman. Lamb had the combination for the outer vault door, but only Hoffman had the combination for the inner vault door.

Martens explained the situation to Smith, who kept glancing out the windows to see if police were coming.

"Just do what's necessary," said Smith.

Martens, Lamb, and Hoffman opened the doors to the bank vault. A padlocked metal money box was removed from the vault and carried by Hoffman and Martens back into the main part of the bank. The money box was roughly eighteen inches long, a foot wide, and maybe ten inches high. It was placed on a counter.

Smith was informed that bank staff needed to find the keys to open the padlocks. He was fine with this and staff rushed to locate the appropriate keys. Most witnesses say Smith was calm and collected during the holdup. They also noticed how thin he was and how pale his arms were. The keys were located and used to open a pair of padlocks on the money box. The contents of the box were emptied into the haversacks.

Crowds gather outside the CIBC Bank at Bathurst Manor Plaza following the "Beatle Bandit" robbery.

"Just put in $100,000. That'll do," said Smith.

Once he was satisfied with the amount of cash gathered, Smith announced that female customers could leave. He ordered them to exit the bank, then head north in the parking lot.

"I've never killed a lady yet and I don't want to start now," remarked Smith.

Male customers were told to leave next. After the men departed, Smith said female bank staff could leave.

Hoffman paused to grab her handbag on the way out.

"I told him I was going to take my cigarettes — that I needed a smoke," Hoffman recalled in court.

Smith let her take her smokes, telling her, "You're very calm, lady."

Smith's haversacks bulged with $25,361.50 in cash. The sacks had straps on the top. Smith put his left forearm through the straps of both bags, balancing them like a shopper carrying groceries. He held the rifle in his other hand.

It was now time for male bank staff to exit, said Smith. The men were told to leave through the front door, then head west, toward a nearby public school. Smith stepped out and walked in the opposite direction, toward the Ford Galaxie parked a block away. He left the guitar case in the bank.

A crowd had gathered in the Bathurst Manor Plaza parking lot, drawn by the sound of gunfire and commotion in the bank. The crowd parted as bank staff and patrons moved through their ranks. Onlookers gawked when Smith appeared, rifle in hand, but gave him a wide berth. Smith glanced behind him a few times as he moved.

Sally Blanc reconnected with her husband, who was enraged. Jack Blanc, wearing a red sports shirt, slacks, tan socks, and black oxford shoes, was in a fighting mood.

"Everyone was standing there. My husband was like, 'Where are the police? Why aren't they here? What's going on? Why are they taking so long? Don't let that man get away,'" Sally Blanc told CBC-TV.

Lepofsky would testify to much the same in a courtroom, although it was clear Blanc's actions were making him nervous.

"When we were out in the parking lot, Mr. Blanc was building himself up, yelling, 'Let's go after him. There's enough of us to take him. There's only one of them. Why should we let him get away?' and this continued … then he started to yell that he was a crack shot and someone get him a gun. [By this point] other people were yelling, 'He is a crack shot! Someone get him a gun,'" said Lepofsky in court.

Lepofsky did not think this was a good idea.

"Myself and several other customers of the bank asked [Blanc] to mind his own business, that the bank was insured. There was no reason for anyone to jeopardize their own lives. The police were on their way. It was up to them and they were trained to handle robbers," said Lepofsky, in the same CBC program that featured Ms. Blanc.

To do nothing but wait was intolerable, however, for "an incorrigible warrior" such as Blanc, said Allan Perly, president of the General Wingate Branch of the Royal Canadian Legion, which the furrier belonged to, during a subsequent television interview. On the witness stand, Sally Blanc admitted that her husband was "quite a character for discipline — maybe he was too much that way, I don't know — but I guess he was not a sergeant in the army for nothing."

Martens walked across the plaza parking lot, then took cover behind some vehicles. Lamb hurried to his 1964 white Comet sedan, parked outside the bank.

"When the bandit went away, I leapt into my car and I was going to follow him, but before I got out of the parking lot, someone else pulled in on an angle and blocked me. So I went back to the bank and got my gun," states Lamb.

At the time, banks in Canada routinely stocked pistols and expected staff to use these weapons in case they were robbed. Smith knew this. When he had pulled one of his earlier armed robberies at a Toronto-area bank in 1960, an enraged bank manager had fired a few shots at him as he sped off in the getaway car. Those shots missed, but he might not always be so lucky.

The CIBC branch kept a pair of .38 caliber Enfield revolvers handy. One of them was in Lamb's desk, the other in the manager's desk. Lamb charged into the bank, snatched the revolver from his desk drawer, and started turning the cylinder. The pistols each had six chambers, but for safety reasons Lamb kept only four loaded. The cylinders were positioned so the hammer would hit an empty chamber if one of the revolvers should fall to the floor.

Under-loading a revolver to prevent an accidental discharge was an old trick that detectives practised when carrying a six-gun in a shoulder holster, but Lamb didn't know that. What he did know, however, was that a colleague at another bank had been killed in a freak accident involving a fully loaded handgun. The bank employee was transporting a basket with a revolver on top when the weapon fell off. The pistol hit the floor, and the hammer hit a live round. The six-shooter fired, killing the unlucky employee. After that, Lamb made sure to keep two chambers empty in both revolvers at his CIBC branch. Cocking the hammer would bring a round into the firing position.

Pistol in hand, Lamb hurried out of the bank and was approached by a furious Blanc.

"What are you all standing there for? Why aren't the police here? Why don't you do something about it? You've all got guns," snapped the angry army veteran.

"He grabbed the gun [and yelled] 'I'm a crack shot! Give me that gun!' I struggled with him over it, to the point where I thought one of us was going to get killed. So, I let go of the gun," recalls Lamb.

Sally Blanc offered a slightly different narrative. Understandable, given the situation and the fact adrenalin was running high in everyone.

According to Sally Blanc, Lamb didn't have a pistol at the ready, but offered to get one for Blanc after he expressed his expertise in firearms. In her recollection, Lamb, or another bank employee, raced back to the bank with Blanc in tow to fetch a weapon.

"I said, 'Please don't do it. Don't do this because my husband will be killed,' I said, 'Don't give him a gun. Please,' and he didn't listen to me. Never answered me or even looked at me," she testified in court.

Multiple witnesses, however, heard Jack Blanc bellowing about being a crack shot and demanding the revolver. There is some discrepancy about Sally Blanc's reaction. Some people said she begged bank staff not to give Blanc a gun. Other witnesses, including liquor store manager Harry Caesar, corroborated Lamb's account.

"Mr. Blanc started to wrestle with [Lamb] and took the gun from him. I heard the accountant say to Mr. Blanc, 'Cock the gun before you shoot it,' and then Mr. Blanc started to run," Caesar told a courtroom.

Stan Lesk recounts much the same. Fourteen years old that summer, Lesk lived with his parents in the Bathurst Manor neighbourhood. The Lesk family were planning to spend that weekend at Stan's sister's cottage in Gravenhurst, Ontario, but first, the family wanted to stop at the Bathurst Manor Plaza to pick up supplies. Lesk's mother went grocery shopping while his father, Bernie Lesk, bought cigarettes at the Bathurst Manor Cigar Store next to the CIBC branch. Lesk tagged along with his dad.

Inside the cigar store, Lesk and his dad "missed the kerfuffle of what happened in the bank. We didn't see any of that," recalls Stan Lesk.

Exiting the cigar store, Bernie and Stan walked into a scene of bedlam. To their astonishment, they saw Jack Blanc — a man they both knew well — yelling about guns and bank robbers as a crowd of people gaped. Bernie Lesk was the swim director at the local YMHA (Young Men's Hebrew Association — the Jewish equivalent of the YMCA), and Blanc was one of his volunteer instructors. Stan Lesk was part of a scuba-diving class Blanc taught.

"I remember seeing Jack grabbing a gun from someone from the bank, and running around the corner," states Stan Lesk.

Blanc ran toward a low-rise apartment building at 118 Overbrook Place at the corner of Elder Street, where Lesk's grandparents lived. Caught up in the turmoil, Stan Lesk raced after his scuba teacher. Lamb, meanwhile, was also shadowing Blanc, staying a few feet behind him.

Today, Stan Lesk describes Blanc as "the bravest guy, to run out of there, grabbing a gun and chasing [Smith]."

Not everyone, however, concurred.

"I ran beside [Blanc] and tried to tell him not to use the gun but throw it away and let someone else try to catch him because I thought he would get killed," Caesar testified in court.

"Oh, he will never bother me. I am a better shot than he is," replied Blanc.

At first, Smith didn't notice the armed customer and accountant rushing toward him. He was too busy trying to start his getaway car. Two days earlier, Smith had stolen the 1963 turquoise-and-white Ford Galaxie from Yorkdale Plaza, a new North York shopping mall. Smith had extensively modified the car, removing the front passenger seat and adding a contact switch to the ignition. The contact switch was supposed to enable Smith to start the car without a key. Sitting in the car with his rifle, pistol, and stolen cash, Smith couldn't get the device to work. The car refused to start.

As Smith fiddled with his contact switch, Blanc came storming up, gun in hand. Lamb followed after the army veteran. Blanc stood behind some small trees for a bit of cover, then aimed his weapon at the Beatle-wigged bank robber. Inside 118 Overbrook Place, a meatpacking plant manager named Robert Lawrence was startled by all the noise on the street outside. He gaped through the windows of his third-floor apartment to see what was going on. In doing so, he got a front-row view of the astonishing scene unfolding below.

From his window, Lawrence observed a man in a strange disguise sitting half in, half out of a vehicle, with a pistol in his hand. Smith had finally noticed Blanc's presence. He fired a round in the air with his .45 but that didn't deter the seasoned ex-soldier. According to witnesses, the antagonists were roughly seventy to seventy-five feet apart. The two military veterans began exchanging shots, and the quiet, suburban neighbourhood exploded in mayhem. Standing behind Blanc, Lamb screamed in alarm. In all the excitement, the bank accountant thought Blanc was firing at the wrong person. But Blanc knew exactly who he was shooting at and blasted away at the bank robber.

In later court testimony, Lawrence spoke of Blanc's shooting abilities: "I noticed a bullet hole in the side of the car," he stated on the witness stand, referring to the Ford Galaxie.

Lawrence and several other witnesses would also remark how enraged Blanc was.

"I will kill the son-of-a-bitch!" yelled the army veteran.

An amazed Stan Lesk watched the action unfold.

"I heard, 'bang, bang, bang'! I jumped to the ground. I saw Jack whaling his gun at him. This was about a block from where I was … There were a number of people there. We went on the ground. I remember looking at the park — everyone was lying down when the shots went off," he states today.

It was a wise move, given that Smith was blasting away with his .45 caliber pistol. Smith shot eight times at the vigilante but none of his rounds hit. When Smith ran out of ammunition, he pressed the magazine release on his .45 and the empty clip fell to the asphalt. Later, Smith would praise Blanc for his bravery and shooting abilities. For now, Smith simply wanted to survive a confrontation with a determined opponent. From behind a low brick wall, Lamb continued to watch the unlikely gun battle.

Blanc got down on one knee on the front lawn of 118 Overbrook Place, an action which would make him a smaller target and allow him to steady his aim. He leveled the revolver, squeezed the trigger and … click. He didn't know the pistol wasn't kept fully loaded. After four shots, the revolver was empty, and Blanc didn't have any replacement cartridges or another weapon. Smith had both. Smith put away his pistol and pointed his FN rifle at the former sergeant. As far as Smith knew, Blanc had more rounds at the ready and was preparing to shoot again. A gun enthusiast with weapons training courtesy of the Royal Canadian Navy, Smith calmly aimed his rifle.

Accounts vary as to Smith's position at this point. In court, Lamb said Smith was still partly sitting in his vehicle, with one foot on the ground, when he switched to his rifle. Lawrence testified that Smith left his car and was standing up when he leveled the FN. Not that it mattered much, given the weaponry involved. The odds had already been stacked in Smith's favour. His .45 was more powerful than the bank-issue .38 revolver and held twice as many cartridges. Both sidearms, however, were intended for close-range action. Now that Smith had switched to his rifle, Blanc stood little chance.

"Any ex-infantry officer will tell you that in warfare, a pistol is so inaccurate as to be almost useless," the *Toronto Telegram* would later note.

This statement needs to be qualified. If indeed the Galaxie took a bullet, that would be evidence of how close Blanc came to hitting the Beatle Bandit.

For all that, Blanc was equipped with a short-range pistol while Smith had a powerful rifle that could hit distant targets on a battlefield. Unlike a machine gun, Smith's .308 FN rifle didn't spray bullets in a continuous stream when the trigger was held tight. It was a semi-automatic weapon, which meant Smith had to squeeze the trigger each time he fired. Following each shot, an empty shell casing was ejected through a side port and a new cartridge was automatically chambered for firing. The box magazine in Smith's rifle contained ten cartridges, each capable of causing devastating destruction.

Even a civilian such as Sally Blanc, standing with the crowd in front of the bank, could sense the street battle had reached a new level of ferocity.

"The first thing we heard; these little shots from the revolver. They were very tiny noises. And then, we all heard this terrible blast from this rifle, and we all knew where it came from. There was nobody else around there with any [weapon] like that," she testified.

Back in the family apartment at 242 Wilmington, young Stanley Blanc was also jarred by the blasts.

"All of a sudden, I hear this 'bang bang bang.' I thought, what is this? Kids used to go to the States on July 4 and bring back illegally these big firecrackers. So that's what I thought, and I look and see people running from the bank," remembers Stanley.

Stanley watched out the window with growing dread. As he well knew, his father was a dedicated and dutiful soldier with a strong knowledge of firearms and military tactics. If the noises outside were in fact gunshots, not firecrackers, he hoped his father stayed far away from the action.

"I thought, please don't let him get involved, because of his experience. I was afraid, if he got involved, he would get killed, and that's exactly what happened," states Stanley.

Stanley couldn't see the gunfight from his window, which was a small mercy given the outcome. When Smith fired his rifle, the shot hit Jack Blanc's right hand, shattering the grip of the bank-issue revolver, and nearly severing his thumb. The bullet continued, striking Blanc in the chest, then penetrating his heart and almost tearing it in half. Bullet fragments entered Blanc's left lung. This wound alone would have killed Blanc, but Smith kept shooting.

"All I saw was a little plume, a flicker, about two-thirds of the way back on the far side of Jack's head. I thought he'd just been grazed," states Lamb.

Blanc hadn't been grazed. The shot blew off the back of his skull, taking with it much of his brain. The Haganah veteran was dead before he hit the grass. From his apartment window, Lawrence saw Blanc lying dead on the lawn. Then Lawrence noticed that his third-floor window screen was coated in blood and brain matter. The shot that killed Blanc was so powerful it had splattered a screen three storeys above. Other onlookers were equally stunned.

"I heard three distinct shots after that and then all was quiet for a few moments and I looked up and I saw Mr. Blanc lying on the grass ... He was dead. His head was blown off at the time," recalled Caesar, who was peeking out from the cover of an apartment building.

Truck driver Jack Cherlon was inside a store at Bathurst Manor Plaza when someone raced in to announce the CIBC branch was being robbed. Cherlon used the store phone to call the operator, telling her to alert police. Then he stepped outside, just in time to witness the gunfight between Blanc and Smith.

"He was aiming at Mr. Blanc and he shot. I could see his head flying right up in the air," Cherlon testified.

Sally Blanc heard someone shouting, "He killed a man! He killed a man!" She raced up the street and saw her husband lying dead between two trees on the lawn of 118 Overbrook Place. She began wailing.

"My husband has been shot!" screamed Sally Blanc hysterically.

Sally Blanc ran toward her husband. When she saw Smith, she went to the ground and played dead.

Smith, meanwhile, was contemplating whether to shoot at Lamb.

"I pointed my gun at the other man. He was moving but I had a deadly bead on him. I held my fire and shouted, 'Halt or I'll shoot!'" Smith later told police.

By the time Smith uttered this command, Lamb was no longer in his sights. Moving fast, Lamb raced back to the bank and called an ambulance from the manager's desk.

"I'm kind of fat and don't run very fast, but I think I probably did that day. I ran back to the bank and got the other gun," states Lamb.

He seized the bank's second .38 revolver and rushed to the vestibule. Lamb stood in the doorway, firing in Smith's general direction. Like a character in an old-West movie, Lamb would shoot, duck for cover, then fire again.

"I shot at him ... I don't think he shot at me, because no glass got broken [in the windows]," he says.

Lamb didn't have much experience with handguns. Shooting six-guns had not been part of his CIBC training, says Lamb.

"I hadn't shot much with a pistol, hardly at all. Maybe only once. But I was a fairly accurate shot with a .22 [rifle]. Back in those days, when I was on my summer holidays, I would take the .22 and go back into the woods, and behind the woods [were] farm fields, and I would go looking for groundhogs," he recalls.

Such experiences were relatively common for boys in that era: "I can't speak to everyone, but don't forget, I was born in 1939 and a lot of other fellows were born after the war was over. A lot of us, our dads hunted. Probably they all hunted — duck hunting or what have you. It was something you grew up with," Lamb continues.

Lamb fired off all four cartridges in that revolver, but none of his shots hit their target. He raced back inside the bank to fetch more ammunition from the storage room. As the accountant searched for bullets, Smith stepped away from the stolen car. It wouldn't start, but Smith was determined not to be taken prisoner.

"I knew I was trapped. I decided not to surrender ... I thought to myself that I must escape or die trying," the bank robber later explained.

Smith began walking back west toward the bank, firing his FN rifle as he moved, to frighten any other would-be shooters. Cartridge casings littered the street.

At this juncture, Cherlon decided to intervene. He rushed up to a man named Duncan Carolan, who worked as a machinist and had parked his car at the plaza before the madness erupted. As Carolan stared at the scene around him, Cherlon approached and demanded his car keys.

"A man just got shot. Let me have your car and I'll go after him!" yelled Cherlon.

Not wanting to argue, Carolan handed over the keys to his cream-coloured 1960 Pontiac. Cherlon jumped in and tore off in the direction of Smith.

At almost the same time, Police Constable Donald Jackson turned right onto Overbrook Place from Wilmington. Constable Jackson was in uniform, but he was driving a blue, unmarked police car. Jackson had been summoned by a call over his radio stating that the CIBC branch at Wilmington and Overbrook was being robbed. PC Jackson was part of the Metropolitan Toronto Police Force — a unified service encompassing the City of Toronto and surrounding communities, including North York.

PC Jackson immediately noticed a large crowd had gathered in the street and the plaza parking lot. People were shouting about a gunman on the loose. PC Jackson pulled the cruiser up to the north side of Overbrook Place.

Lepofsky spotted the car and yelled, "There's a gunfight down the street!"

The constable hit the accelerator and raced up Overbrook. Then PC Jackson saw the shooter — a weird-looking guy in a strange disguise standing in the street, pointing a rifle at him. Smith was poised less than twenty feet from the startled cop.

PC Jackson slammed on the brakes, then ducked below the dashboard. This might have seemed less than heroic, but the constable was considerably outgunned. Smith fired three shots at the police cruiser. Two rounds blasted the windshield, sending shards of glass into the constable's face, while a third shot blew out the left front headlight. The flying bits of glass cut the constable's face as he lay on the car floor.

"The policeman didn't have a chance to stop his car completely or get out of the car when the bandit started firing at him," Lepofsky later stated in court.

Into this chaos came Cherlon, driving his borrowed Pontiac down Overbrook. While Cherlon had planned to chase Smith, he realized he was now directly in the line of fire. The rifleman who had just shot up a police car was right in front of him. Cherlon dived out of the Pontiac, leaving the keys in the ignition. The driverless car continued to lurch forward. It rolled a few feet, then hit the curb on the south side of Overbrook and came to a stop.

Smith was quick to sense the rather incredible opportunity that had just been handed to him. Had a screenwriter included such a scene in a crime movie, they probably would have been called out for creating such an unbelievable scenario. This was real life, however, and Smith commandeered the Pontiac, tossing his cash-filled haversacks into the back seat and his rifle onto the front. Then he jumped into the driver's seat and left.

According to witnesses, Smith didn't tear away from the scene as might be expected. With Blanc lying dead on the ground, a police cruiser full of bullets in the street, and dozens of shocked onlookers, Smith drove slowly up to Elder Street, then went north.

"I got in the car. I assumed the policeman was still capable of combat. And I knew all hell had broken loose this time. I still figured my number was up, but I decided not to panic in fear of death. I reloaded my pistol, perhaps my rifle. I had gone this far, and I still was not going to be taken alive. I didn't see any reason to rush … because I felt I must face fate. I had never been in such a gunfight as this before," Smith later recounted.

Inside his shot-up cruiser, PC Jackson could hear people shouting, "He's getting away! He's getting away!"

Cherlon opened the door of the bullet-pocked car and saw the constable, lying on the floor, covered in bits of glass.

"He's right here, right in front of you! Go and get him!" yelled Cherlon.

The constable staggered out of his police car and was informed that Smith was driving away on Elder Street. Jackson got back in his cruiser and tried to make chase. His windshield was shattered, and his car damaged by bullets. The cruiser quickly conked out. The constable tried to call in for help, but the radio wouldn't work either. It, too, had been damaged in Smith's fusillade.

By this point, Lamb had retrieved more cartridges and wanted to resume firing from the bank doorway. He looked about and realized Smith was gone. Lamb stepped away from the bank toward Blanc's devastated body. The top of his skull was almost completely shot away. Lying near Blanc was a .38 caliber revolver with a shattered grip.

"I looked into the back of his head, and there was nothing in it," recalls the bank accountant.

Stan Lesk also caught a glimpse of Blanc's corpse. When the shooting stopped, his mother and father grabbed him and raced into 118 Overbrook Place to see if the Lesk grandparents were safe. Like many people in the neighbourhood, Stan's grandparents were Holocaust survivors.

To the relief of their family, the Lesk grandparents were alive and uninjured, if badly shaken. Ignoring his parents' order not to look, Lesk went to the balcony of his grandparents' apartment to observe the scene.

"I looked on the balcony. [Blanc] was about twenty-five, thirty feet away from me on the other side ... I saw the body. He was lying on his side, with one leg bent, like he was going to the chiropractor, but I knew his face was shot off," states Lesk.

For all his bravado, Lesk was "terrified. Shaking like a leaf. A fourteen-year-old kid, seeing this."

As a mass of people gaped in shock, PC Jackson also stepped toward Blanc. His face bloodied, the constable noticed a sobbing woman sitting on the sidewalk. The woman was calling out, "My husband. My husband," over and over. The constable made sure Sally Blanc wasn't injured and tried to console her. Then PC Jackson used a telephone in the Bathurst Manor Cigar Store to call the radio room at Metropolitan Toronto Police headquarters. After giving a quick update about the situation, the constable stepped outside to interview witnesses. Other police were now pouring into the area. Sally Blanc managed to pull herself together and identify the body to police.

Detective Sergeant Roderick Marsh was among the first lawmen to arrive after Smith fled. In court he described the crime

Police detectives search for shell casings and other evidence following Jack Blanc's murder.

The chaotic crime scene following Jack Blanc's murder. Blanc's body, covered in a sheet, is on the ground to the right.

scene as "utter chaos" with large crowds milling in front of the bank and 118 Overbrook.

Marsh ordered a constable to guard Blanc's body, then began speaking to witnesses. He noticed there were two abandoned vehicles at the scene — PC Jackson's bullet-ridden cruiser and the failed getaway car. Walking carefully to avoid stepping on cartridge casings on the road, the detective sergeant examined the ditched Ford Galaxie. There was a carton and several scattered dollar bills inside the car, and the front passenger seat was missing. Det. Sgt. Marsh didn't touch the vehicle and left it where it was. The Galaxie and other cars would be taken to a police garage for closer inspection. Det. Sgt. Marsh began taking measurements of the crime scene and recording other data.

A total of twenty-five shots had been fired during the melee. Blanc and Lamb fired four rounds each with the remainder coming from Smith, who was now driving off, having successfully robbed another bank and eluded the law, for now.

At roughly 6:15 p.m., a detective from the Criminal Identification Bureau arrived to take crime-scene photographs. Fifteen minutes later, Coroner Doctor Murray Naiberg inspected Blanc's remains and officially pronounced him dead, a finding that was hardly a surprise given his condition. Some men arrived from the "Toronto Removal Service," as a police report put it, and placed Blanc on a stretcher. His body was driven to the City Morgue on Lombard Street.

Police and the curious continued to flood into the area, along with reporters.

"Police came and my dad was interviewed by the police because he was one of the people to identify the body … My grandparents were pretty freaked out. They were pretty upset, but we went on with our lives. I literally went back into our car an hour later. We were in the car, going up north [to Gravenhurst]," states Lesk.

Stunned members of Blanc's family, including his daughter, Diane, spoke with the press.

"It's a terrible thing to say, but I'm not shocked by the way my father was killed … It was a compulsion … He was a sergeant again and he had to get into it …. I was stunned at first but when I heard how it happened, it just seemed typical of Dad. He was a good dad. He was a hard worker who never shirked," Diane told the *Toronto Daily Star*.

The shootout marked "Jack Blanc's last heroic stand. He was a very brave man," added Al Perly, a couple days later in the *Globe*.

By any standard, Lamb had also performed heroically, risking his life to fire at the Beatle Bandit.

Looking back, Lamb won't acknowledge he did anything particularly courageous: "It could have just been a knee-jerk reaction. I'm not a particularly brave guy," he states.

He was admittedly annoyed, however, by the barrage of questions from police.

"At some point, police took me down to the station. I'm going to use the word interrogate because that's what they did. I was getting really annoyed, because it was almost like good cop, bad cop. The point of it was, they were trying to get all the facts straight. They had to unmuddle some of my thinking. After it was all over, I don't know how long it took me, I realized what they did was absolutely proper to try to get the story straight," recalls Lamb.

After giving his statement, Lamb returned to his workplace, which was now crowded with bank staff, police officers, and others.

"I remember going back to the branch. I come walking in, and of course, it's full of people. I come walking in, trying to speak up to someone and I just broke down, and bawled my eyes out," he says.

◆ ◆ ◆

Back in the apartment at 242 Wilmington Avenue, a fourteen-year-old boy maintained an anxious vigil for his parents.

"I pretty well thought something had happened because I was waiting and waiting and waiting. Going back and forth [to the window] and looking. I was listening to the door to be opened. We often left our door wide open to let air circulate. I was waiting to hear my parents come up the stairs. I heard the door open. Someone asked, 'Is that Butch?' I said yes. He said, 'Your mother will be here in a minute.' It was two homicide detectives," remembers Stanley.

Chapter Two

Boy to Man and Madness

As a child, Matthew Kerry Smith was tall, slim, and strange. He was born in Winnipeg, Manitoba, on January 22, 1940. His parents always called him Kerry.

Kerry's father, Matthew Bartley Smith, was born on July 23, 1909, in St. Paul, Minnesota. His family moved to western Canada when he was a child and he attended the University of Saskatchewan, graduating with a degree in science. Commonly known as Matthew or "Matt" Smith, he worked as a journalist in Moose Jaw, Saskatchewan. There he met Helen Isabel Crichton and fell in love. She was born in 1911 in Moose Jaw and worked in that city as a schoolteacher. While legal documents and city directories identified her by her first name, people generally called her Isabel or "Belle," for short, and that is how this book will refer to her.

Matt Smith and Isabel married on July 29, 1932. They lived in Moose Jaw for a while, then moved to Winnipeg, where they had two children. Their first child — Belle Lianne Smith — was born October 21, 1936. Kerry arrived two and a half years later.

When the Second World War broke out, Matt Smith stayed in Canada and continued to work in journalism. In 1941, Matt Smith and Isabel moved with their two small kids to Willowdale,

Ontario. In a letter to his parents dated March 5, 1942, Matt Smith offered a glimpse of family life during this period. After a humorous description of Lianne's attempt at preparing dinner, he wrote, "Kerry is talking quite a bit now. Only when necessary, it is true, but he manages to put the right words together, rather tersely, as if he were paying for them by meter."

In Ontario, Matt Smith worked as an editor for the Canadian Broadcasting Corporation (CBC), the national network of radio (and later television) stations. He also wrote freelance articles on the side on a wide variety of topics. A Matt Smith feature in the August 1944 edition of *Magazine Digest* detailed a type of artificial respiration used to revive sailors rescued after ships were sunk by German U-boats. Three months later he had an article in the same publication entitled "How to Crash and Live," examining airplane and automotive safety issues.

More moves ensued and family life continued apace.

Isabel had psychiatric problems and her struggle with mental illness deeply affected her son, who was terrified he would inherit her condition. She would fluctuate between periods of relative lucidity and others of almost debilitating illness, to the point of needing hospitalization. In later years Isabel would be diagnosed as schizophrenic.

If his personal life was in tatters, Matt Smith blossomed in his chosen career. He bought a 102-acre farm in Cooksville, a community outside Toronto, and worked hard as a CBC Radio editor.

In 1949, when Kerry was nine and his sister twelve, they were sent to live with their grandparents in Coderre, Saskatchewan, near Moose Jaw. It seemed a healthier environment, given Isabel's condition.

Matt Smith launched divorce proceedings, requesting custody of his children. The divorce documents listed August 1, 1950, as the official day he and Isabel separated, although the marriage had crumbled long before then. Taking note of the situation, a Family

Court judge decided the kids would be better off with their father for the time being.

"After the judge told me I was going to have the kids, I decided that, all right, if I was going to do it, I would do it right … I was so busy trying to make my way in the world that I didn't have much time for children and didn't know much about how to handle them. So now that I was going to have to, I went and saw some psychiatrists and psychologists and asked them how," said Matt Smith, in a subsequent interview with Scott Young for the *Globe and Mail*.

The experts Matt Smith consulted stressed the importance of providing children with love, attention, and a sense of justice. Having absorbed these lessons, Matt drove to Saskatchewan to pick up Kerry and Lianne. By all accounts, Kerry was upset. He would describe the months spent with his grandparents as the happiest in his life. A smart kid who loved to read, Kerry did not like being uprooted.

Matt Smith tried to bond with his kids during the long car ride back to Cooksville. The more he talked with his son, the more unsettled he felt. Things came to a head during a detour in Minnesota.

"We started out driving east and I decided we'd do it slow and easy so I could get to know the boy better. We had some relatives in St. Paul, and we decided to break our trip there. Then, I noticed that he'd pick up a newspaper and he'd say, 'Look at this thing — LOOK! The fools!'" Matt Smith told Scott Young.

Kerry was reading an article about a bank robbery. The little boy thought the thieves were idiots because they were caught. The robbers should have wiped off their weapons to get rid of fingerprints and been alert to the presence of marked bills in the loot, said the boy. If they had been more careful, the crooks wouldn't have been captured, he asserted.

Matt Smith tried to ignore his son's remarks. Lots of kids talk about cops and robbers and are interested in guns and crime. But Smith Senior soon realized his boy was obsessed.

"After a couple of days, when all he would talk about was how the crooks could get away with this bank job, my hair started raising on end," recalled Matt Smith.

A hard-working, conventional man, Smith Senior did not admire criminals.

"Finally, I began talking to him, explaining this was not the way he had to look at it. Trying to explain the thing from the viewpoint of morality and society," he stated.

The lesson seemed to work, at first. Kerry stopped critiquing the stratagems of bank robbers. A much relieved Matt Smith finished the drive home, and the kids decamped at his Cooksville farm. Within a few weeks, Kerry started rambling once more about dumb crooks, to the dismay of his father.

Matt Smith did his best to adjust to family life as a single father. A document signed by his son (writing as Kerry Smith), dated March 11, 1952, outlined a series of chores the boy was responsible for. The note, witnessed by Matt Smith, read as follows:

I, Kerry Smith, hereby solemnly agree that, in return for making an airplane trip to London, Ontario, with my dad, I will carry out the following duties faithfully:

1. Clean out all the junk in my room, and once more put the stuff I am not sure about in boxes in the locker.
2. Wash the supper dishes regularly.
3. Take out the garbage each day.
4. Clean the rug on week-ends.
5. Tidy the newspapers each day.
6. Write an acceptable 200-word report on the trip.

This promise to remain in full force until the end of June this year.

Ironically, the chore list included the line, "I also certify that I am of sound mind, and that no force was used in making me agree to these terms."

The ensuing report, titled "My First Airplane Trip," contained some astute observations by Smith about riding in an airplane.

"Within minutes the propellers of our plane started to buzz harder and harder; then they slowed down as the brakes were released. Then they started to go faster and faster until we were airborne, going up slowly, passing farmhouses which were quite big at the time. Later, we saw that they were not big but as small as ants," wrote Smith.

At some point in the early 1950s, the family moved from Cooksville to a five-room apartment on Bathurst Street in North York. Matt Smith had left the world of journalism to try his luck at business. He was now running a company called Allied Manufacturing that made paints and chemicals.

The company was listed in the business section of the 1954 edition of the Toronto City Directory under the category "Chemicals— Manufacturers." "Matt B Smith," living at 3815 Bathurst Street North and working at "Allied Mfg Co" is listed in the residential portion of the same directory. This marked the first time Matt Smith's firm was mentioned in the city directory, which used past-year information. If Matt Smith's correspondence is anything to go by, his firm was already operating prior to being cited in the directory.

In a letter to his parents dated August 18, 1951, Matt Smith mentioned some new products under development including "a copper-base concrete paint, a leak stopping compound and a wood putty." On the family front, Matt Smith was busy raising his kids, with the help of a part-time housekeeper.

"So far we have got along swell, through division of work among the three of us," wrote Matt Smith, of his children.

In the same letter, Matt Smith discussed how he broached the topic of divorce with Kerry and Lianne. This involved telling the kids "how the judge and later the psychiatrist had said that the children would be better off in a one-parent home where there was

Matthew Kerry Smith as a boy.

no quarrelling [and] that Belle too would be better off if she were free of this tension," wrote Smith Senior.

The children were told that "they were deeply loved by both of us, and that, in fact, it was only this love for them, this determination to protect them even at expense of ourselves, that had kept Belle and me together for several years," continued the letter.

Interestingly, Matt Smith also stated, "With this load off his mind, Kerry's nightmares immediately vanished."

Smith Senior didn't offer any further details about these bad dreams but did write that his son was working for his firm a couple days a week at 50 cents an hour.

As part of the divorce process, an investigator from the Children's Aid Society (CAS) of York County visited Matt Smith and his children in June 1952. The investigator, who also met with Isabel, was supposed to evaluate conditions in each household. The findings would guide the court as it pondered a permanent custodial arrangement. The investigator's report was included in Matt Smith's divorce documents.

According to the CAS inspector, "there appears to be a good relationship between Mr. Smith and the children. Housekeeping standards are good."

The furnishings in the Bathurst Street apartment were "modern, clean and comfortable." As for sleeping arrangements, "girl has own room. Boy shares room with father," wrote the investigator.

Fifteen-year-old Lianne was described as "an attractive, slender girl with [a] pleasant outgoing manner … She is a responsible reliable girl and Mr. Smith states she presents no behaviour problems."

Kerry, who was then twelve, "is a slight lad with a friendly attitude and good health. He attends Summit Heights Public School and is in grade seven. He too is doing well in school. He is interested in sports. Like his sister he appears to be happy and well-adjusted to the home situation and is willing to do his share in the home," added the report.

Isabel also came across relatively well in the CAS document.

"She is at present employed as an office worker for the T. Eaton Co., although she has no office training. She states she is in good health. She states she enjoys sewing and music. She smokes but states she does not drink. Mrs. Smith, from one brief interview, indicated she felt it was necessary to 'impress' the investigator," wrote the examiner.

For all that, the report clearly favoured Matt Smith: "It would appear that Mr. Smith is endeavouring to give his children love, affection and a rounded out family life as far as possible when there is no mother in the home. He has hopes for both children to go to university and he is financially able to undertake this," stated the CAS summary.

Documents in Matt Smith's divorce file indicated he was earning $100 a week (worth nearly ten times as much today, factoring inflation) and faced weekly expenses of $92, including rent, food, clothes, and $15 a week to his wife. Smith Senior had real-estate and business holdings with a combined value of $25,000 (nearly a quarter-million dollars by contemporary standards). The report also noted that he "owns and operates the Allied Mfg. Company (Chemical Specialities)."

Isabel's assets came to $55, including $25 in a bank account. Her weekly income was $47 ($15 from her husband and $32 from work).

When the divorce was finalized, Matt Smith was officially granted custody. This proved a mixed blessing, as Kerry became stranger and harder to reach. His father bought him a guitar when the boy expressed an interest in learning to play. Kerry was grateful and started practising. A colour photograph taken at the time shows a fresh-faced Kerry, happily plunking away at what appears to be a C-chord on his acoustic guitar. Kerry is beaming; a happy, handsome kid. He quickly lost interest in the guitar, however, and stopped practising, never touching the instrument again.

Kerry took up a new hobby. He became immersed in the amateur "ham radio" community. A low-tech precursor of the internet, "ham radio" networks allowed individuals to communicate with each other over long distances using mini radio "stations" in their homes.

Matt Smith acquired books, parts, and a radio kit for his son. Kerry built a receiver and transmitter and then wrote a test to get licensed.

"He became the youngest amateur radio operator in Canada. They had to pass a fairly stiff test, Morse code, theory in radio and so on like that. And they couldn't write it until their fifteenth birthday. He wrote it on his fifteenth birthday," stated Matt Smith, in his Scott Young interview.

After passing the test, Kerry lost interest in amateur radio and dropped it as a hobby.

Smith was not close to his sister, or anyone else for that matter. He had few friends and seemed content to be unsociable. Smith later told psychiatrists he felt an intense sense of sibling rivalry, and felt that Lianne, who excelled in school, was the preferred child.

Kerry's mother might have offered the boy emotional support but had her own demons to deal with. She didn't live with her kids, and Kerry had little contact with her.

Matt Smith contacted a mental health association for advice about his son. He outlined the family situation and was given the name of a psychiatrist who could speak to his troubled boy. When Matt Smith relayed this news to his son, he did not take it well. Kerry burst into tears and said, "You mean I'm going crazy just like my mother?"

Kerry did meet with the psychiatrist, but he wouldn't respond to questions. Even without his participation, the doctor concluded that Kerry was deeply disturbed and told his father as much.

"He was inscrutable. You knew there was something going on inside his brain, but you never knew exactly what," recalled Matt Smith.

Adding another layer of complexity to the family dynamic, Kerry Smith developed an intensely competitive streak with his father.

"The psychiatrist told me that the two underlying motives in his life were first of all that he despised his mother because she was mentally ill and second his desire to compete and surpass me," said Matt Smith.

Smith Senior pointed to a time he talked to his son about his future. The teenager said he wanted to run a farm outside Toronto, just like dad, only his farm would be ten times bigger. Instead of being offended, Matt Smith offered some practical advice. Maybe Kerry could work for a farmer or take agricultural courses at

Matthew Kerry Smith in the Royal Canadian Navy.

college? His son scoffed at these sensible ideas and told his father he would simply hire outside workers to do the actual labour on his dream farm. How Kerry would pay for all of this remained unclear.

Despite being highly intelligent, Kerry did poorly in school. Over his brief academic career, Kerry Smith was a student at Armour Heights Public School, Third Street Public School, Downsview Collegiate, and Lawrence Park Collegiate. Seeing his boy struggle, Smith Senior put him in a private boarding school for grade nine.

The school was called Pickering College, though it was based in Newmarket, Ontario. It had an impressive pedigree, having been founded by Quakers in the 1840s and moving to its Newmarket location in 1909.

Matt Smith hoped the environment might prod his son to focus on his studies. The plan didn't work. Kerry repeated grade nine and continued to have difficulty with his lessons. Matt Smith hired tutors, to no avail. The tutors told him he was wasting his money; his son just sat there during lessons, staring blankly, not participating.

Kerry never passed grade ten — a source of great bitterness and shame later in his life. The otherwise bright kid dropped out of school and remained distant from his well-meaning father. He attended Pickering until June 1957, then looked for work.

Kerry took a job with a company called Reilly Locksmith. Matt Smith was initially pleased, but his delight soon turned to dismay. He discovered his son was using his newfound talents to pick locks around the family house. Matt Smith kept documents locked up in filing cabinets. Kerry began picking the locks and opening these private cabinets — for no other reason than he could.

In the summer of 1957, when Kerry was seventeen, he began working part-time for his father at Allied Manufacturing. At the same age he also had his first known run-in with police, being pulled over for speeding. Police caught him driving at 70 mph without a licence. He was fined $28.

In fall 1957, the high-school dropout came up with a new plan: he would join the Royal Canadian Navy (RCN).

Matt Smith wasn't pleased. He wanted his son to complete his education. Since Kerry was under eighteen, he required his father's consent to join up. Smith Senior contacted the headmaster at Pickering College for a chat. The headmaster pointed out that Kerry would be eighteen in less than a year, at which time he could join the navy without parental consent. It was a compelling argument and Matt Smith grudgingly signed a consent form, allowing his son to apply for the RCN.

Kerry was given a physical examination at HMCS *York*, a naval base in Toronto. His enrolment form states that he was five eleven tall, weighed 141 pounds, and had blue eyes, brown hair, and a medium complexion. His previous occupation was listed as "factory help" at Allied Manufacturing, and the United Church was given as his religious denomination.

A medical report noted that Kerry "wears glasses occasionally for distant vision." A chest X-ray revealed no signs of tuberculosis. When asked if he ever experienced "nervous trouble," Kerry answered no. He did answer in the affirmative when asked, "Has any member of your family suffered from nervous or mental trouble?"

December 24, 1957, marked Kerry's first day of enrolment in the navy. He was given the service number 39150-H and entered the RCN as an ordinary seaman in the communications radio group. His enlistment was supposed to last five years, until late 1962.

Initial training was conducted at HMCS *Cornwallis*, a sprawling base near Halifax, Nova Scotia. In the roughly fifty years it was in operation, over half a million personnel were trained at the facility. According to a Government of Canada history, the base was the biggest naval training centre in the British Commonwealth during the Second World War.

At first Kerry's new career move seemed to be working out.

"Quite evidently, the navy life agrees with you, and I am so glad," wrote Matt Smith, in a letter to his son dated February 10, 1958.

In the same letter, Smith Senior discussed some pocket books he planned to send his son and offered details about work and family life. Matt Smith was now doing real-estate transactions, on top of his role at Allied Manufacturing.

"I've been working real hard. Got six new products out, doing all the copy and artwork myself, and worked 28 hours without sleep at one stretch in order to make a printer's deadline. Then, I slept for 30 hours ... Sold two lots up at the hill by myself and have turned the selling over to another real-estate company," reported Smith Senior.

In another letter from the same period, Matt Smith touched on his son's decision to join the navy: "I'm glad you like it there. You'll find an entirely different type of life than you have ever known, a life of challenge and opportunity, in which the outcome will be entirely up to you," he wrote.

Matt Smith's letters to his seaman son are mostly upbeat. One missive did mention an encounter Smith Senior had with a former classmate of Kerry's from Pickering College. The classmate apparently passed on some news about Kerry's peers, which Matt Smith included in his letter.

"At least seven of the boys in your class are here in town, either at other schools or at work; they found the atmosphere at Pickering too sociable and as a result flunked out. So, you weren't the only one who found the climate there was not [conducive] to proper study," he wrote.

Smith Senior occasionally alluded to money problems. In one letter he thanked Kerry for sending him some cash. Matt Smith would later become wealthy through his business dealings, but that was in the future.

Smith also corresponded with his mother, who mailed him a series of handwritten letters expressing maternal concerns and comments about her day-to-day life. Isabel's neatly penned notes, signed "Mother" or "Belle Crichton," are generally short but cogent.

"I miss just having you near to be able to say hello but it is a good thing to get started right in life and no doubt the navy will be good," stated one letter.

Isabel was well enough to travel on occasion, and one letter referenced a visit she made to her hometown.

"Arrived in Moose Jaw after a pleasant ride on the 'Canadian.' It is a new train which they tell me cost $5 million to build … Hope you are enjoying your training and that along with the hard work you are enjoying life. Write and tell me how you are getting along. Love Mother."

Kerry's naval career continued apace.

His special qualifications were listed as "swimming, skating, chess, basketball, amateur radio," on a Divisional Record Sheet dated September 1958. The same document said he scored 70 percent in parade, 79 percent in seamanship, and 61 percent for final achievement. In a handwritten report, an HMCS *Cornwallis* officer described Kerry as "an average man in all respects. His hobby is amateur radio which he seems very proficient with." Under the category "general impression" Kerry received a "passable" ranking.

During his time at HMCS *Cornwallis*, Kerry became pals with a fellow sailor named Richard Skey. The friendship would continue after both men left the navy — though not in a positive way for either man.

Following training Kerry was posted to HMCS *Cap de la Madeleine*, a vessel dating from the Second World War. Categorized as a "river-class frigate" in naval terminology, the *Cap de la Madeleine* was designed to fight German U-boats in the Atlantic. Ships in this class were fast, well-armed, and roughly three hundred feet long, with a thirty-six-foot-seven-inch beam and a displacement of 1,440 tons. River-class frigates were typically crewed by 10 officers and 135 ratings.

The *Cap de la Madeleine* had entered service in late 1944, escorting a convoy of supply ships to Great Britain. During the journey the ship developed mechanical issues and had to return home for repairs. Once the vessel was fixed, it was decided the ship would be prepped for battle in the Pacific against Japan. This prep-work was cancelled when Japan surrendered.

After the war, the RCN sold the ship to a private company but then reacquired the vessel for its own use. Recommissioned in 1954, the *Cap de la Madeleine* served up and down the eastern seaboard, patrolling North American waters.

Smith's uniform from the *Cap de la Madeleine* has been preserved by family members. It consists of dark blue pants with the name "M. Smith" stitched on the inside in red capital letters, along with his serial number. A matching dark blue jacket also features his name and serial number in red. The jacket bears a Canada patch and other shoulder emblems as well. On the *Cap de la Madeleine*, Smith also wore a brimmed, beige-coloured sailor's cap with the ship's name emblazoned on a blue stripe at the bottom.

Kerry soon tired of naval life. He went absent without leave (AWOL) from the *Cap de la Madeleine* for six days in July 1959, ostensibly to visit family. When he returned to duty, he was fined $72.90 and given fourteen days detention. When questioned, Kerry complained that routine navy work "made him nervous and depressed" and was eager to be discharged, stated a report.

An unimpressed superior on the HMCS *Cap de la Madeleine* gave Kerry a dismissive review. Kerry's attitude and demeanour had deteriorated "to the point where he can no longer be relied upon as an effective member of the ship's company," wrote the officer in mid-1959.

While stationed at the HMCS *Stadacona* barracks in September of that year, Kerry was hospitalized for over a week with infectious hepatitis. Through bedrest and medicine he recovered, but his attitude didn't improve.

"Able Seaman SMITH appears to have lost interest in Communications work and in the NAVY generally," noted an assessment from September 1959.

Kerry wanted to leave the RCN and contacted his father to intervene. At the time, Matt Smith was enjoying a period of bliss with his son away from home.

"These years were rather peaceful for me because this was a very traumatic thing to live with. A kid that you know, you feel that there is something wrong," recalled Matt Smith.

Matt Smith had a keen sense of parental duty and wrote to his son's commanding officer, asking him to release Kerry with an honourable discharge. In return, Matt Smith expected his son to resume his education.

The letter did the trick. It helped that the Royal Canadian Navy was fed up with Kerry, whose eccentric mannerisms were attracting notice.

"This man was interviewed to determine suitability for retention in the service. At the time of the interview, he was very ill-groomed. His hair was untidy, and his nails were bitten and dirty and his shirt was grimy. He spoke very rapidly, constantly moved his hands, squirmed in his chair, and presented a rather strange affect at times," stated a naval report.

Smith was dismissed on October 15, 1959, with an honourable discharge.

Kerry never properly explained why he wanted to quit. When pressed, he said navy life was boring and that his fellow sailors drank too much. In later years, Kerry offered a few additional insights about his naval service to a Metropolitan Toronto Police detective, who repeated these comments in court.

"He said that he enjoyed the basic training and the ballistics course ... [However, he] thought that our navy was so out of date that they were not capable of defending the country," testified Detective Robert Dougall.

Kerry made another major life decision in this period. He decided he no longer wanted to be called Kerry. He asked people to refer to him by his first name, Matthew. His family, however, continued to call him Kerry. For the sake of continuity, this book will now call him Smith.

Beyond his name change, Smith didn't know what to do next with his life. He moved into the basement apartment occupied by his mother at 31 Glenforest Road in north Toronto. The house was owned by Matt Smith, who rented units to other tenants. Isabel is listed at this address in the 1960 Toronto City Directory under the name Isabel Crichton. Future directories would sometimes use a variation of her married name ("Isabel Smith").

The living arrangement was not ideal for a young man concerned about his own sanity. Isabel was erratic and eccentric. Convinced there were microphones scattered about her apartment, she blasted her television and radio at full volume to prevent any eavesdropping. She was phobic about germs and sometimes stared trancelike at her television, convinced she was engaged in telepathic two-way communication.

For all this, Smith managed to get his life back on track, briefly. His father was delighted when Smith signed up for Toronto Matriculation College to resume his education. Smith worked hard, for a while. He passed his Christmas exams but quit the college early in the new year, as he tried to figure out his next move.

During this same period, Smith complained about debilitating physical ailments.

"After he came out of the navy, he had a splitting headache. Now this headache was almost constant. He'd bend over in agony with this headache. He told me he'd had the headache continuously for over six months, ever since he'd been in a brawl in a bar in Halifax and got whacked over the head with a beer bottle," Matt Smith told Scott Young.

In addition to the bar fight, Smith offered another explanation for the headaches. At sea, his ship would sometimes roll in heavy weather, Smith recalled. If he was sleeping in his berth when this happened, the sudden movement sometimes caused his skull to slam against the bulkheads.

As a seaman, Smith had been subjected to regular physical examinations. Doctors noted that he was myopic, but if they found evidence of brain damage it wasn't mentioned in their reports.

Matt Smith arranged for his son to be examined by civilian doctors. Smith was given X-rays and tests by physicians, who found nothing obviously wrong like a skull fracture or a tumour.

As with many things in Smith's life, the precise nature of his head injuries remains a mystery — if they happened at all. After seeing the doctors, Smith said the headaches went away on their own. Even so, he continued behaving in strange ways.

Shortly after his discharge, Smith showed up at his father's place driving a Buick in good condition. To his surprised father, Smith said the car cost $2,100 — a lot of money for someone who had just left the navy, hardly a high-paying profession. When asked how he could afford such a slick vehicle, Smith said he had earned extra money selling liquor to his fellow seamen in the naval barracks.

Being a businessman, Matt Smith was impressed by son's entrepreneurial spirit. He later conceded that his son's account of being a bootlegger might have been a lie, maybe to cover for darker criminal activity. Selling alcohol did seem out of character for someone concerned about the drinking habits of his navy comrades. Then again, "Don't get high on your own supply" is a common adage among drug dealers.

Smith remained a loner, with few close friends or romantic relationships. He would later complain about his inability to crack jokes or socialize on a one-on-one basis. If inwardly tormented, Smith's outward appearance was impressive. Smith was a handsome young man, with a tall, lean physique, honed by military exercise. When he wore glasses he looked like a young executive on the rise, not an aimless veteran.

Smith took a job in a factory but soon found a more rewarding vocation. He decided to rob a bank. It would be a fulfillment of childhood fantasies about bank heists. Smith planned things carefully. After finding a suitable target in the form of the Imperial Bank of Canada in Parkwoods Plaza, North York, he needed a getaway vehicle.

Smith stole a Pontiac sedan from the Bloor Street West car lot of West Side Pontiac Limited on February 5, 1960. The vehicle was a company car left at the lot by a salesman who didn't remove the keys from the ignition.

On the morning of February 9, Smith drove the stolen Pontiac to the Parkwoods Plaza, at Parkwoods Village Drive and York Mills Road. He parked the car, then strolled through the front door of the bank, brandishing a .32 caliber automatic pistol and a khaki-coloured haversack.

It was 11:00 a.m. and there were no customers in the bank. The only people present were manager Douglas Dunning, teller/accountant Colin Beales, and ledger-keeper Isobel Lunn. Smith walked up to Beales's wicket, pistol in hand. He slapped the canvas bag on the counter and shouted, "Fill it up!"

At this point, the bank robbery turned potentially deadly. Smith's .32 automatic discharged, and the shot hit Beales in the head.

The bullet "glanced off his forehead, ricocheted off a wall and flattened itself in the ceiling of the branch office," reported the *Globe and Mail*. Beales collapsed, bleeding and unconscious, on the bank floor.

At the sound of the shot, Dunning and Lunn also dove to the floor. The bank manager hit a silent holdup alarm.

Smith would later deny that he deliberately shot the teller. Even police gave him the benefit of the doubt: "Det. Insp. Bernard Loveridge believes the gunman did not mean to fire, but was so nervous he accidentally pulled the trigger," wrote the *Telegram*.

Smith might have regretted the accidental shooting, but it didn't put him off his mission. He ignored Beales and leapt on top of the bank counter. Waving his .32 for effect, Smith ordered the two non-comatose employees to stand up.

Dunning and Lunn warily got to their feet. Smith ordered Dunning to go into the bank vault and retrieve the cash. The manager informed the wannabe holdup man that two combination safes needed to be opened before any money could be had. The two safes could not be opened without the help of Beales, added the bank manager. And Beales was currently lying unconscious on the floor.

Unable to seize the money in the vault, Smith demanded the petty cash from the tellers' cages. In the predigital era, bank tellers routinely stocked large amounts of paper money and coins. Smith ordered the bank manager to scoop up cash and place it in the canvas bag. Smith grabbed the bag, now filled with $3,008, exited the bank, and raced to his stolen Pontiac.

The bank manager wasn't through. With his teller/accountant lying injured on the floor, Dunning seized a revolver from a desk drawer. He raced outside and fired a few shots at the disappearing Pontiac. None of the rounds hit the target. Police later found the Pontiac ditched in a church parking lot in Brampton, Ontario.

"The bandit was described as between 25 and 35 years old, 6 feet tall and about 135 pounds. He was wearing a white cap and a dark three-quarter length topcoat," stated the *Globe*. The *Telegram* added that the holdup man had a "thin build, fair to pale complexion, with a long thin face and high cheek bones."

Beales was rushed unconscious to Toronto East General Hospital. Doctors operated, removing part of the bullet that was still wedged in his skull. He was treated for a compound skull fracture, and surgeons dealt with a blood clot.

The *Telegram* ran an article about Beales's young fiancée. Eighteen-year-old Valerie Kennard was said to be praying for the recovery of her partner-to-be. The pair were planning to be married in London, England.

Beales was transferred to Toronto General Hospital on February 20. A metal plate was implanted in his head and remained there the rest of his life. Beales spent another two weeks in recovery, then was sent home to heal. Following a three-month at-home convalescence, he went back to work at the bank.

Smith, for his part, used the cash he took from the robbery to pay for a trip to Western Canada.

No one knew he was responsible for the Parkwoods Plaza

robbery until years later, after he robbed the Bathurst Manor CIBC branch and fired a gun again, this time to lethal effect.

It wasn't all violence and robbery for the young naval veteran, however. He had an unexpected reunion with old navy buddy Richard Skey, who was now in Toronto. The encounter took place sometime in late 1959 or early 1960 — Skey wasn't sure of the exact date.

"I was coming out of a show downtown and I happened to bump into him on the street and we started seeing each other," Skey later testified.

The former naval pals had plenty in common. Skey, too, had left the service early, due to "psychiatric problems," as he told a courtroom. Skey was also a criminal, who would rack up nine auto theft-related charges by the early 1960s. Skey and Smith would become close companions, as the latter's fascination with guns and bank robbery grew into an all-encompassing obsession.

Chapter Three

Pistols and a Car Chase

Matthew Kerry Smith pressed harder on the accelerator of the Oldsmobile until he was travelling at seventy miles an hour along city streets. It was a year after the Parkwoods Plaza holdup, and Smith, pursued by a line of police vehicles, was driving so erratically startled motorists pulled over in alarm. He raced through residential neighbourhoods, past homes and businesses, through five stop signs and two red lights.

Smith had planned the Imperial Bank job with a degree of care and caution. Shooting the teller had been unintentional, as he later acknowledged. This car chase, by contrast, was a spontaneous gesture of wild abandon.

Smith, who by now was again working for his father at Allied Manufacturing, had started the evening in his own car, as usual, commuting to his job from the Glenforest Road apartment he shared with his mother. But, driving back to the apartment on the night of February 9, 1961, Smith decided to change his car. He parked and then began walking the cold sidewalks, searching for a new vehicle. He found an Oldsmobile with the keys in the ignition and helped himself.

For someone driving a stolen vehicle, Smith didn't exactly keep a low profile. After spotting a police car on Fairlawn Avenue, Smith turned off his lights and swerved as if to smash into the cruiser. A collision was avoided, but the startled constable at the wheel called for backup. Backup arrived, a chase ensued, and at one point five police scout cars and a motorcycle were in hot pursuit. The motorcycle cop was forced out of the chase after swerving onto a residential lawn, causing $150 in damage.

The police tailed the errant Oldsmobile for three miles, then the chase abruptly ended when Smith slammed into a vehicle at Redpath Avenue and Eglinton Avenue East. Police cornered Smith and hustled him off to a local station. It had been a year since Smith held up the Imperial Bank of Canada, but police didn't know he was responsible for that. The cops simply thought they had nabbed an unusually reckless driver. Smith was placed behind bars and charged with criminal negligence and auto theft.

Matt Smith was oblivious to his son's actions until someone asked if he'd seen a newspaper article about a weird car chase in north Toronto. Smith was missing work, which puzzled his father. After reading the article and making inquiries, Smith Senior realized why his son hadn't been showing up for his shifts.

"I went up to the police station and the policeman who arrested him said, 'There's something wrong with the boy … This kid wanted to be caught,'" said Matt Smith in his interview with Scott Young.

On February 10, Smith appeared before Magistrate Thomas Elmore, who struggled to make sense of the case. Smith told the justice he stole the Oldsmobile because someone had stolen his car. This wasn't true and would seem a strange excuse even if it were.

"Why did you do this?" asked Magistrate Elmore.

"I wanted to get away from the police, because I had stolen the car I was in," explained Smith.

"And what should I do with you?" asked the magistrate.

At this point, Smith chuckled and said, "Throw the book at me."

This, Magistrate Elmore declined to do. Smith was remanded and kept behind bars for sentencing on February 27. Despite Smith's cavalier attitude, the justice let him off easy. Smith was put on probation for eighteen months and told to get evaluated at the Forensic Clinic of Toronto Psychiatric Hospital. Of course, Magistrate Elmore had no idea Smith had robbed a bank the year before.

Established in 1956, the Forensic Clinic was the go-to place in Toronto to send criminals who displayed signs of mental illness.

"Offenders who have committed minor but apparently sense-less crimes — such as Matthew Kerry Smith's car theft — can be sent there for pre-sentence examination. If found guilty, they can be given suspended sentences or placed on probation — on con-dition that they regularly attend therapeutic sessions at the clinic for the period of their sentence," explained a 1966 feature story in *Maclean's* magazine.

The *Maclean's* timeline appears to be wrong — Smith visited the clinic after being sentenced, not before. Like all new patients, Smith was assessed by an intake committee made up of psycholo-gists, psychiatrists, social workers, and the like. Dr. Ronald Stokes, a graduate of the University of Toronto medical school, chaired Smith's intake conference.

Smith was interviewed and analyzed, then the committee dis-cussed his case among themselves. They concluded that Smith suf-fered from schizophrenia. Usually manifesting in late adolescence or early adulthood, schizophrenia scrambles thoughts and percep-tions, causing confusion, delusions, and hallucinations. In severe cases, it can so reduce a person that they can barely function.

People with schizophrenia "are said to have a psychosis, which refers to an inability to test reality, in other words, to separate what is real from what is fantasy," Dr. Stokes later stated in court.

While it was a damning diagnosis, Smith benefitted from good timing.

Wearing glasses and a suit, Matthew Kerry Smith resembled
a young executive on the rise, not an aimless veteran.

A few years earlier, a criminal ordered into treatment might
have faced a highly abusive therapeutic regime. Psychiatric treat-
ments in North America during the 1950s included ice baths,
insulin therapy (patients were overdosed with insulin, to induce
a coma), electro-shock therapy, and lobotomies. In a lobotomy, a
doctor poked an icepick or another sharp instrument up a patient's
eye socket and wiggled the pointed end around in their brains.
Supposedly, this would make a patient more tranquil, but usually
it reduced their mental capacity or put them into a vegetative state.

By the early 1960s, these horrors were being phased out and
replaced with less brutal forms of therapy and antipsychotic medi-
cations such as Thorazine.

The intake committee decided Smith didn't need to be institutionalized. They felt he wasn't dangerous, and his condition could be best treated on an outpatient basis. This opinion was probably shaped by practical considerations, given there was a long waiting list for hospital beds in psychiatric institutions at the time.

Dr. Stokes later testified that he believed Smith would require "some form of hospitalization in the not too distant future."

For the moment, however, Smith was told to take outpatient treatment at the Toronto Psychiatric Hospital. These treatment orders weren't strict, however, and Smith soon abandoned therapy. There were no repercussions, although his father, already angry about Smith's car thievery, was furious.

"I asked him later, 'Why did you do this?' He didn't have any explanation for it. It was just as if he had to do it. He had to get out of his car and get into somebody else's car and steal a car," Matt Smith told Scott Young.

Smith Senior's concern was compounded by a strange phone call he received at the office. He was informed that the sample of titanium he had ordered was available. Only, Matt Smith hadn't ordered any titanium. A little sleuthing revealed that his son had placed the order.

When asked why he wanted titanium, Smith told his father, "I thought I'd like to look at it."

Smith eventually obtained his titanium sample and ordered more. The bill, which came to his father's office, amounted to hundreds of dollars. Smith was fascinated by titanium: he later tried to fashion a bulletproof vest out of the ultrahard metal. At the time, Smith Senior thought his son's interest in titanium was just another of his eccentric whims.

At this juncture, Smith suddenly confounded his father by getting his life back on track. Smith went out West in 1962, taking a job in Thompson, Manitoba, at a mine run by the International Nickel Company (better known as "Inco"). Smith toiled at an Inco mine for a year and a half, earning a reputation as a solid, reliable worker.

With his wages, Smith bought handguns and enjoyed target shooting in his off-hours. Smith also travelled to Indigenous settlements to party. In a less-enlightened era, his association with First Nations people raised eyebrows. He also appeared to have changed his opinion about alcohol and now indulged occasionally. In his navy days, Smith had frowned on excessive drinking.

Smith became friends with an Inco co-worker named Joe Bashutzky. They didn't have long to pal around, however, as Smith returned to Toronto in May 1963. He took a job at a tire manufacturer. Newspaper and police reports identified the company as the "Dunlop Rubber Company" or "Dunlop Tire Company." The firm is listed in the 1964 Greater Toronto City Directory as "Dunlop Canada Ltd.," in downtown Toronto.

Though gainfully employed, Smith remained unpredictable and eccentric. He dropped in on his dad every three months or so, usually with no advance warning. Matt Smith dreaded these visits because his son wouldn't engage in normal conversation. Smith would give a bare-bones summary of what he had been up to and otherwise seem inattentive and spacey.

His father noticed another disconcerting development. While Smith's navy acquaintances were mostly clean-cut types, he was now hanging out with a scruffier, seedier group of friends. Among other activities, Smith enjoyed firing weapons with his new pals.

"He would come out with his guns. And I would say, 'No, look, please. I don't want you shooting guns, I don't believe in guns.' He would say he wasn't killing anything; they were just going out for target practice. When I heard these guns go off it was almost as if these bullets were going through me," Matt Smith told Scott Young.

Later, psychiatrists would suggest Smith was trying to mould himself into the model of a mighty warrior. He also remained furiously competitive with his father. Once, Matt Smith purchased a tape recorder for business dictation. To his great surprise, Smith promptly went out and bought a more expensive tape recorder, for no apparent purpose other than to one-up his dad.

Matt Smith said the Forensic Clinic wouldn't share its findings with him. It was obvious, however, that his boy wasn't receiving the help he needed.

Sadly, Matt Smith had good reason to be alarmed. His son's warrior-man posturing would soon take a dangerous turn.

♦ ♦ ♦

On Sunday night, December 8, 1963, caretaker Alfred Bonnici was working in the boiler room of the Denison Armoury at Highway 401 and Dufferin Street in North York when he encountered an intruder.

It was a time of year when most people were focused on the Christmas season — buying presents, arranging parties, and planning dinner menus. The intruder had other thoughts on his mind.

The man who broke into the armoury was clad in "a tweed type topcoat, covered with a grey plastic raincoat and a khaki coloured balaclava over his head," according to a police report. The intruder held a briefcase in one hand and a pistol in the other.

Holding his hostage at gunpoint, Matthew Kerry Smith said he wanted to steal some weapons to rob banks. It was around 7:30 p.m. and the beginning of a very strange night for caretaker Bonnici.

In his quest for military-grade guns, Smith had chosen well. As run by the Department of National Defence, armouries then and now are locations where reserve units gather to train and parade. Armouries also house offices for military headquarters, and weapons.

After subduing the caretaker, Smith began rambling like a movie villain who tells a temporarily helpless hero all about his evil plans. Smith boasted about his bank-robbing abilities and familiarity with firearms, noted a police report.

Smith did, however, reassure the caretaker that "there was nothing political in his motives and that he was not a member of the FLQ," added the report.

At the time, the Front de libération du Québec had just kicked off a violent campaign for Quebec independence. The terror group would achieve infamy in 1970 when it kidnapped British trade commissioner James Cross and Quebec deputy premier Pierre Laporte, triggering a national crisis. During the early 1960s, the FLQ was content to let off bombs in Quebec, which was terrifying enough.

While gabbing, Smith produced a second pistol, which he held in his left hand. He now toted a revolver and a semi-automatic pistol.

Much as he liked handguns, Smith wanted bigger and better weapons. Smith told the caretaker he was interested in Fabrique Nationale (FN) semi-automatic rifles and Sten guns. Sten guns were simply-built submachine guns used in the Second World War by Canadian and British troops. They weren't very accurate but had the advantage of being small and easily concealable, making them an ideal weapon for robbing banks.

Smith stopped rambling and ordered the caretaker to pry open the door to a storage room. He handed Bonnici a crowbar he had brought with him for just this purpose. While Bonnici struggled with the crowbar, Smith fired one of his pistols. It wasn't clear if this was an accidental discharge or a deliberate warning shot to scare the caretaker. The bullet hit a lock on one of the storage doors but didn't hurt anyone.

The noise drew the attention of Major C.J. McCombe, a militia officer working in an office upstairs. The major raced to the boiler room and was surprised to see a burglar with two guns holding the caretaker hostage.

Smith produced handcuffs and secured Bonnici and Major McCombe to a steel railing on the front stairs of the armoury. He told the men to hand over the keys to any storage rooms containing Sten guns or money. His prisoners said they didn't have them. Smith considered his options and decided a strategic retreat was in order. He told the men not to call police, then left the armoury, his mission a failure.

Half-an-hour later, cleaner Ammanuel Zarb showed up for his shift. Zarb discovered Major McCombe and caretaker Bonnici handcuffed to a railing. Police were contacted and the incident widely reported in Toronto newspapers. No one had a clue about the identity of the unsuccessful gun thief.

During December, Smith also took the time to socialize with his old navy buddy, Richard Skey.

Skey, who was spending Christmas 1963 at his father's house, was pleasantly surprised when Smith contacted him. The pair had been seeing each other sporadically since their reunion in Toronto. Smith invited his navy pal for some Christmas cheer. Skey accepted the offer and visited Smith at the 31 Glenforest Road basement apartment. While glad to see Smith, Skey was wary about Isabel, whose moods and attitude could change abruptly.

"She was always a strange woman. I mean, one minute she would be very, very happy to see me and the next minute she would say, 'Get out,'" Skey would later tell a courtroom.

Smith seemed in good spirits, however. Unfortunately, he was running low on cash. If Smith wanted to buy Christmas presents, he needed to acquire more money. So, he set out to rob another bank.

The target was the Toronto-Dominion Bank at 2793 Bathurst Street at Glencairn Avenue. Around 9:30 a.m. on December 24, Smith stole a 1959 Volkswagen from a VW dealer at Weston Road and Eglinton Avenue West. As with the Oldsmobile he took for a joyride, someone had left their keys in the ignition of the Volkswagen.

Smith drove the getaway car to 31 Glenforest Road. He parked and went inside to prepare his disguise and gather weapons.

Smith put on a grey, hooded track shirt, dark pants, and yellow sunglasses. From his growing collection of guns, Smith selected a 9 mm Browning automatic pistol and a revolver. Smith packed his weapons in a khaki haversack, which he placed in the Volkswagen. In midafternoon of Christmas Eve, he drove to the parking lot of the TD Bank. Smith parked and exited the vehicle. It was just a few minutes before 3 p.m. when Smith entered the bank, the lower part of his face concealed by a blue scarf.

Smith removed his handguns from the haversack and stepped to the centre of the bank. He pointed the Browning at the ceiling and fired a shot, immediately commanding everyone's attention. With a pistol in each hand, Smith ordered the bank manager out of his office. The manager and the two customers he had been chatting with complied and stood before the gunman.

Smith handed his sack to a customer and told him to fill it with cash. The flustered customer passed the sack to a teller. Smith ordered the teller to fill the sack with cash from the till, which the teller proceeded to do. Smith assured those present he didn't intend to hurt anyone. He wouldn't to hesitate to shoot, however, if need be.

The bag was passed along a row of tellers, each of whom filled it with more cash. A clerk named Robert Fraser took the bulging bag, now containing $12,155.91, and handed it to Smith. All male customers and staff were ordered to exit by the front door and head north on Bathurst Street. Smith followed the procession, last in line. It suddenly occurred to Smith that it was the day before Christmas.

Smith bellowed, "Merry Christmas!" to the startled staff, then hurried to his getaway car. He shoved his guns and bulging haversack inside and took off, driving east on Glencairn Avenue. No one from the bank tried to shoot at him this time.

Smith drove to Lawrence Plaza, at Bathurst Street and Lawrence Avenue. He ditched the Volkswagen and transferred the cash and guns to his own car, previously left in the lot. Then he drove off, having completed his third successful bank heist.

Smith used some of the proceeds to buy Christmas gifts. He also made plans to buy himself a present. Early in the New Year, he headed out to purchase this gift, which he had long coveted.

◆ ◆ ◆

Stanley Willison looked up as the customer entered Hallam Sporting Goods at 621 Yonge Street, a couple blocks north of Wellesley Street. Located on one of downtown Toronto's busiest streets, the store sold guns and ammunition, among other items. It was roughly eleven in the morning on January 10, 1964.

Much later, when asked on the witness stand about this customer, Willison admitted he couldn't remember what the man looked like.

"I would judge him to be around twenty-five to thirty years of age," the salesman testified.

Beyond that, the salesman drew a blank. He couldn't even identify the customer in court.

If the patron's appearance was nondescript, his manner was precise and determined. He told Willison he wanted a Fabrique Nationale 7.62 mm semi-automatic rifle.

"I looked up on the shelf and there wasn't one in stock, so I went to the back room and fetched one," Willison testified.

The salesman found the rifle in question and brought it back to the customer. The model selected was black in colour, bore the serial number 2562, and had a vertical magazine near the trigger guard.

Somewhat to Willison's surprise, the customer didn't want to look the rifle over, even though it was a relatively expensive item.

The customer said he was familiar with that weapon so there was no need to inspect this one.

Willison started filling in paperwork. When asked, the customer said his name was Owen Fox. He gave his address as 19 West Ridge Drive. Once these formalities were out of the way, Matthew Kerry Smith paid for the rifle in cash. With tax, the bill came to $220.42 (worth about 8.5 times as much today, given inflation).

Smith didn't need a permit to buy the weapon, and the store wasn't required to perform a background check before selling it to him. Hallam Sporting Goods wasn't even required to pass on details about the transaction to a national gun registry like the one run now by the RCMP.

Willison completed the paperwork that was required of him. The sales slip was marked "one 308 Browning serial 2562." Willison filed away a copy of the invoice, and Smith stepped out of the store, proud owner of a 7.62 mm FN military-style rifle.

Smith had broken into an armoury and failed to find any FN rifles, but managed to purchase one perfectly legally at a gun store on Toronto's main street.

While delighted to finally have his coveted FN rifle, Smith received bad news from another front a few weeks later. He was laid off from his job as a machine operator at Dunlop Rubber. The layoff had less to do with his performance than with the plant's bottom line. There wasn't sufficient work to keep the plant fully staffed, so Smith was let go.

Smith took his dismissal in stride. He still had plenty of cash from the TD robbery, so he decided a vacation was in order. Smith packed a few things in his 1949 Oldsmobile, then headed out west to have some fun and see old friends.

Things didn't go quite as planned: in Manitoba, Smith's car got stuck in the snow (a common road hazard during prairie winters). Smith contacted his old Inco pal, Joe Bashutzky, for help.

"I got a phone call. I was not at home at the time. There was a Mr. Smith that wanted to see me, so I drove out to where he was … I believe it was in Erickson, Manitoba, and he come back with me and stayed overnight at my place," Bashutzky would later tell a courtroom.

The men drove out the next day and rescued Smith's Oldsmobile from the snow. After that, the pair travelled around the province for a few days. When Smith announced he was returning to Toronto, he said Bashutzky was welcome to join him.

"[He] asked me if I would like to come along for a holiday as I was doing nothing, I was drawing Unemployment Insurance. I said I wouldn't mind for a few weeks," testified Bashutzky.

There would be a third person in the car making the journey back to Toronto.

Her name was Eileen Charity Griffiths, and she was Smith's new girlfriend.

Chapter Four

Love and Bank Robbery

E ileen Charity Amiotte was born January 30, 1944, the fourth
child of William Amiotte and Charity Bone. In a handwritten entry on Eileen's Notice of Birth issued by the Province of
Manitoba, her father is described as "French half-breed." Under the
categories "racial origin of father" and "racial origin of mother" a
clerk wrote "Indian" in both cases. The condescending bureaucratic
language is evidence of the narrow-minded world Eileen was born
into.

William Amiotte hailed from North Dakota and worked as a
trapper, according to his daughter's Notice of Birth. His marriage
to Eileen's mother was his second. William Amiotte had two children from his first marriage and would have nine with Charity,
including Eileen. The Amiotte family were Métis, a community
descended from French settlers and Indigenous Peoples in Western
Canada.

Eileen's official birthplace was listed as "Keeseekoowenin
Res Elphinstone." Elphinstone was a tiny community in southern Manitoba while "Res" meant reservation — more accurately,
the home territory of the Keeseekoowenin Ojibway First Nation.
Eileen ended her schooling after fifth grade and was married in

1962 to Gerald Griffiths, "an Englishman living in Minnesota, near Elphinstone," according to the *Telegram*. Eileen was eighteen at the time of her marriage. The couple had a daughter, Estelle, born April 13, 1962, but the marriage didn't last. Eileen and Griffiths separated in late 1963: she kept her husband's last name.

By early 1964, with her separation behind her, Eileen wanted to have fun. When her friend Evelyn McKay suggested a night on the town, Eileen eagerly accepted. McKay was dating Joe Bashutzky, who was hanging out with his old pal, Matthew Kerry Smith. McKay offered to set up Eileen with Smith and she agreed. So, on Saturday night, February 8, McKay, Bashutzky, Eileen, and Smith set out on a double date.

Photographs of Eileen from this period show an attractive, dark-eyed young woman, with brunette hair. The *Star* would run a picture of Eileen looking stylish in a knee-length winter coat, her hair cut collar length.

Smith was clearly taken by her. More remarkably, she seemed equally attracted to him. While tall and handsome, Smith wasn't exactly a charmer or a lady's man. He obviously possessed some appeal, however, because Eileen uprooted her life at his suggestion after a single date. When Smith asked, Eileen agreed to travel to Toronto to live with him. She left Estelle in the care of her mother and headed off with her new partner.

"I met [Smith] on a blind date a few months after I'd broken up with my husband ... Matt was just passing through. Next day we were on our way to Winnipeg and Toronto," Eileen later recalled in an interview with the *Telegram*.

Bashutzky, out of work anyway, joined the couple. With roughly $10 to his name, he was eager to make a fresh start. Smith proved to be a most generous host, paying for everyone's expenses on the road.

Once the trio made it to Toronto, Bashutzky went to stay with his brother. He alternated over the next few months between places of his own and his brother's residence. Eileen moved in with

Smith — a daring move in a more puritanical time when couples didn't typically cohabitate before marriage.

At first Eileen and Smith stayed at 31 Glenforest Road. Given Isabel's psychiatric problems and the cramped quarters, it was probably not an optimal living arrangement. The young couple soon found other quarters, at a hotel called the Glenview Terraces at 2900 Yonge Street. The hotel would eventually be demolished and the site — like much of older Toronto — would be transformed by construction. Where the hotel once stood there is now an upscale condominium building called The Residences of Muir Park, with some units priced at over a million dollars.

Smith was called back to his machinist job at the Dunlop tire plant. Bashutzky also found a job there but still had money problems. Bashutzky borrowed funds from Smith on occasion, though later he would insist he paid most of it back.

Smith could afford to be munificent because he was temporarily flush. With the combined proceeds from his December bank robbery and pay cheques from Dunlop, Smith had enough money to buy a house. His choice of residence was a bungalow at 213 Byng Avenue in the suburban neighbourhood of Willowdale. He put a down payment on the $17,000 home in March.

Willowdale was located between Bathurst Street and Bayview Avenue near Highway 401, in what is now the northern reaches of Toronto. Smith had lived in Willowdale for a short time with his parents in the early 1940s, in a period when the family moved frequently around the Toronto area. It was a tranquil neighbourhood filled with family homes.

"The original housing stock built in the 1940s and 50s consists of charming bungalows and pretty brick 2-storey homes," states the website Neighbourhood Guide.

The home Smith purchased would soon feature prominently in pictures splashed across Toronto newspapers. In these images, 213 Byng Avenue appears to be a pleasant, nondescript abode. A pair of windows flank a main central door at the front of the house. Inside, there were four bedrooms, a basement, and various living spaces.

Richard Skey was recruited to help move furniture into Smith's new residence and assist with renovation.

"I helped him decorate it, repaint it. It wasn't in too good a shape ... we repainted the house completely," Skey later stated in court.

Even repainted, the interior of the bungalow remained somewhat sparse. There wasn't much furniture, though Smith did acquire a big freezer for the basement and a television for a ground-floor room. Reading material was also available, and not just the gun magazines Smith was fond of. A *Telegram* reporter who toured the bungalow the following year spotted a bookshelf containing an eclectic choice of titles. These included "several books on speed writing, an auto repairs manual, a book on theatrical makeup, a cookbook, a file of recipes and household hints, an anthology of American poetry, a text on Television, Writing and Selling."

Perhaps to reward Skey for his help in renovating his new home, Smith invited his friend to move in. Skey was fine with that and was occupying a bedroom by April. He shared space in the bungalow with Smith and Eileen (Estelle was still being cared for by Eileen's mother back in Manitoba).

Smith appeared to be on the right track. He was working again at Dunlop, had a girlfriend and a home. His father struggled to keep track of all the changes in his son's life.

"He was out in western Canada and suddenly he came back with this girl, Eileen Griffith [sic]. He said now that he had a wife, he was going to get a house. So, I was told he was renting the house, but later I heard he bought the place, for $17,000," stated Smith Senior, in his interview with Scott Young.

Matt Smith was taken aback to discover Eileen was still married to another man but came to appreciate her.

"Not a bad little woman, an underprivileged woman and with a sweet little child," he noted, in his interview.

If Smith Senior grudgingly accepted Eileen, he worried about his son's finances. Even though Smith was working hard at Dunlop, his father wondered how he could afford a $17,000 home while supporting a live-in partner. Matt Smith sensed there were things going on in his boy's life he didn't know about.

Smith Senior was right to worry, given that his son was stockpiling weapons and working on his marksmanship. When he wasn't watching television with his housemates or tinkering with cars outside, Smith liked to shoot guns in the basement. Smith "wanted to become a crack shot," Skey told a courtroom.

Sometimes Skey joined in, and the men plinked away at targets with pellet guns or .22s. These were not powerful weapons, but Skey was fully aware that Smith had plenty of other, more dangerous firearms haphazardly stashed about. At one point, Smith owned between twenty-five and thirty guns, some of which he kept under his bed.

The hobbies and habits of the new residents at 213 Byng Avenue did not go unnoticed. After the home became notorious, a neighbour told journalists she "often heard guns being fired next door at all hours of the night."

The neighbour, identified as "Mrs. Ross Hancock" by the *Toronto Daily Star*, wasn't particularly perturbed by this. Her husband liked shooting guns, too. Mrs. Hancock was more annoyed by the lack of social graces shown by the new occupants of the bungalow.

"They were awfully strange people. We tried to make friends in a neighbourly way, but they never said more than 'hello' to us … They weren't friendly, yet they had lots of people coming and going in cars. They kept the strangest hours," Mrs. Hancock told the *Star*.

If he wasn't eager to chat with the neighbours, Smith was extremely voluble within the confines of his new home. When not otherwise occupied, Smith had taken to ranting at his house guests. These rants, which could go on for hours, usually centred on government oppression and the need for violent revolution.

"We stayed up various nights, talking until the wee hours … He was against the government, the way it was being run," said Skey on the witness stand.

While in favour of radical change, Smith was vague about how his postrevolutionary world would function. He was fascinated by the dynamics of armed revolt but had little interest in ideology. Smith did say he would settle for running the police or army, come the revolution, but that was about as specific as he got. If Skey had any opinions about such matters, he generally kept them to himself.

"We just discussed — well, he discussed. I was just sitting there listening most of the time, and he was fed up with the way the government was being run," said Skey in court.

In an interesting twist of family history, Eileen's paternal grandfather was named after Louis Riel, arguably Canada's most famous rebel. On two separate occasions in the nineteenth century, Riel led uprisings of the Métis people against the Canadian government. These rebellions were crushed, and Riel was hanged, becoming a martyr to his supporters in the process.

Having a relative named after a famous rebel and putting up with lengthy tirades from your boyfriend are two different things, however. On the witness stand, Eileen confessed she "didn't really listen" to Smith's rants and had no idea what he was talking about.

This no-nonsense attitude fits with descriptions of Eileen from other people. Eileen didn't leave behind much writing of her own, and her adult contemporaries are either quite old or dead. Some newspaper articles contain comments from Eileen and public records chronicle snippets of her background. Still, little has been written about Eileen as a person.

Estelle Griffiths said her mother was "very friendly, very warm," a view echoed by Cindy Griffiths.

Through marriage, Cindy became Eileen's daughter-in-law in the late 1980s. She described Eileen as "to the point" and "very gruff," but warm and kind once people got to know her.

In one of the few media interviews Eileen did, with a *Telegram* reporter in 1965, she spoke glowingly about Smith. The *Tely* described her as "the brunette daughter of a French father and Indian mother," who "smiled and dimpled as she told of her romance with Matt."

"We've been happy. He had a lot of respect for me and I'd say Matt is a gentleman. I didn't mind living common-law with him … Estelle knows too, even at her age. She's been crying for her daddy — that's what she calls Matt. He treats her just like she was his. Some people who live common-law don't get along with the child of the other person but with this one it was different," stated Eileen.

Eileen said Smith "treated her better than anybody ever had ever treated her," added Cindy Griffiths.

For all that, Smith could be domineering.

"I do remember [Eileen] saying that she was not supposed to go into the basement [at Byng Avenue]. She never questioned that. She was told not to, and it didn't bother her. It was not her place to go. He had his friends, and she was never allowed down there. She said it never bothered her," states Cindy Griffiths.

This was contradicted by other witnesses who said Eileen did take part in target practice and other activities in the basement. Smith did, however, later express some primitive sentiments about gender relations to police.

Smith remained a highly supportive partner in other ways. In June 1965, Smith bought Eileen a plane ticket so she could visit her family in Manitoba and have a reunion with her daughter. At times, Smith said the CIBC robbery was motivated in part to raise funds so he could buy a house for Eileen. This was supposedly to provide her with some stability because he was concerned with her sometimes excessive drinking.

During this period, Skey enrolled in a training initiative for the unemployed that saw him taking classes at the Provincial Institute of Automotive and Allied Trades.

As Eileen visited family and Skey learned new skills, Smith began plotting a new bank robbery. Sure, he was making decent wages at Dunlop, but between buying the bungalow and supporting other people, his funds were getting low. Smith's intended revolution would require more money than he could earn doing overtime. Smith had carried out two bank heists to date. Aside from almost getting shot by an irate bank employee and wounding a teller himself, these robberies had been successful and profitable.

Smith set about picking his weapons and a disguise for the new heist. He hit on the notion of making a bulletproof vest out of titanium, the hard metal that had long fascinated him. Having previously acquired titanium through the subterfuge involving his father's company, Smith passed a sample to Skey. He asked if his friend could bend it at the Institute of Automotive and Allied Trades.

"I took a square piece, approximately 12 by 12 inches, and I took it to the school … They have a body shop, and they have a lot of metal bending equipment such as rollers where you can roll it through and if it is a piece of normal tin or something like that you can make a stove pipe out of it," said Skey in court.

Skey got permission from his course instructor to bend the sample using machine tools at the training facility when class was done for the day. Presumably, Skey didn't mention that the titanium was going to be used for a bulletproof vest. In any case, the instructor thought the titanium was too tough to bend and he was right. The machine tools he used were not up to the task, Skey told a courtroom.

Police would later find a homemade titanium bulletproof vest at 213 Byng Avenue. This suggests that either Smith managed to work the metal himself or that Skey was more successful than he was willing to admit.

Smith gave Skey additional responsibilities as well.

"There was a costume he asked my advice on — a couple of various costumes. One of them was with a Beatle wig on and a sweater and a sweatshirt on top of this sweater was more or less to hide the [bulletproof] vest … And a couple of other [costumes], all of which I more or less told him I thought they were stupid looking and that he should, you know, forget it," testified Skey.

Apparently, the decision to wear a CKEY T-shirt for the heist reflected a rare attempt at humour on Smith's part. According to Skey, Smith was amused by the thought of an armed bank robber wearing a T-shirt with the slogan "Good Guys."

Skey took a job as a truck driver for Bowden Lumber and began chauffeuring Smith around the city, looking for getaway cars to steal. Smith had his friend drop him off at Yorkdale Plaza in North York on one occasion when Smith carried a gun inside a violin case just like a Hollywood hitman. Going armed in public wasn't anything new for Smith.

"Matt carried a gun quite often," Skey explained in court, just "not necessarily in a violin case."

Skey left his friend at the mall, then went about making deliveries for Bowden Lumber. When his workday ended, Skey returned to Byng Avenue. He discovered that Smith was already home. Smith ruefully announced he hadn't been able to find a car that suited his needs.

A few days later, Smith decided to take a drive himself and bring his friend with him. As Skey sat in the passenger seat, Smith drove a 1953 Ford to the Bathurst Manor neighbourhood. He had found a bank in this area and was thinking about robbing it.

Bathurst Manor was an unlikely locale for Smith's next rampage. The community was a quiet subdivision on the northern outskirts of what was then North York and is now Toronto. Built on farmland in the 1950s, the neighbourhood bordered Finch Avenue in the north and Sheppard Avenue West in the south, with the Don

River marking the eastern boundary and Dufferin Street the western. There were farms and dusty rural roads nearby and a sense of isolation from bustling Toronto. Like Willowdale, it was a peaceful, family-oriented place.

Globe and Mail arts and architecture critic John Bentley Mays described Bathurst Manor as an "area of quiet, broad streets" filled with suburban-style homes.

Once he entered the Bathurst Manor neighbourhood, Smith drove to a shopping centre at Wilmington Avenue and Overbrook Place. Smith looked around, "pointed out a bank and he said, 'This is the bank.' I am not sure of the words he used, but he used words to the effect that, 'This is the bank I am planning on robbing,'" Skey later said in court.

The unpretentious, two-storey shopping centre that drew Smith and Skey was called the Bathurst Manor Plaza. Opened in 1957 to serve the local community, it contained about twenty businesses. These included the CIBC bank, Bestway Cleaners Ltd., William Hair Styling, an LCBO (Liquor Control Board of Ontario) outlet, Bathurst Manor Shoe Repair, a grocery store, cigar shop, bakery, etc. As one of the only retail hubs in the area, the plaza was the commercial heart of the neighbourhood.

"Everything was focused on Wilmington Park and the plaza. I never, ever saw the outside of Bathurst Manor; my mother didn't drive and most of [the mothers] did not drive," said long-time Bathurst Manor resident Judi Cohen in a *Globe and Mail* profile about the neighbourhood.

Stan Greenspan, who grew up in Bathurst Manor and was nine years old in 1964, echoes this view.

"It was one of the first areas where we had a plaza right in the midst of a development. People only had one car in the family — mother would give you a dollar and say, 'Go get some milk and bread.' You got on your bike and go. [The plaza] really was the centre of the area," stated Greenspan in an interview.

As the only bank in the plaza, the CIBC branch was particularly busy. It was the only place to deposit a cheque or withdraw cash from your account. Online banking was decades away.

Working at the CIBC branch, accountant Carman Lamb was in a good position to observe the denizens of Bathurst Manor.

"It was a Jewish community. One of the things that sort of gives you an odd feeling when I saw it — I noticed more on the ladies then the men, when they came in with summer dresses on, with short sleeves [there were] tattoos on their arms. Numbers tattooed on their arms," said Lamb.

Numbers tattooed by Nazi officials at concentration camps during the Second World War.

In the presence of such clients, "[you] developed a lot of empathy," added Lamb.

"There was a very high percentage of Holocaust survivors. Many came to Canada after they were able, in the early 1950s, when Canada opened up. It was to the point where I was one of the few people who had four grandparents. Many of my friends had no grandparents at all," noted Greenspan.

Other Bathurst Manor residents had moved from "the crowded, ramshackle Kensington Market area, which for almost a century, had been Toronto's famous, first landing spot for immigrants" in the downtown core, wrote Mays.

Given such demographics, Smith had the cockeyed notion that the CIBC bank would be packed with cash.

"The area was a Jewish area — and he was figuring that there should be a fair amount of money in this bank," Skey told a courtroom.

While happy to listen to Smith's plans, Skey wanted no part in the actual robbery. Nor did he report his friend to police. Skey stayed silent because of fear and a misplaced sense of loyalty, he later claimed. For all that, Skey had no problem accepting stolen money from Smith, knowing full well where it came from.

As Skey was discovering, being friends with Smith could be a challenge, and not just because of his propensity for armed robbery. "You could never tell what he was going to do next. I mean he would be happy and 'buddy-buddy' one minute, and five minutes later he would be a grouch and you could never figure him out," Skey told a courtroom.

Toward the end of July, Smith sourced a suitable getaway car at Yorkdale Plaza in North York. The vehicle was a 1963 Ford Galaxie hardtop, left in the parking lot by a man named Andrea Ackarman, who was shopping at the mall with his wife. When Ackarman returned to the parking lot, he discovered his car was missing. He reported the disappearance to police.

Ackarman would later testify that he had locked the doors and taken the key out of the ignition of his vehicle before it was stolen. Of Romanian background, Ackarman was not fluent in English and struggled at times to make himself understood during his court appearance. His statement would indicate, however, that he didn't leave his doors unlocked or his keys in the ignition like previous victims of Smith's car thefts. This was corroborated by Deputy Crown Herbert Langdon, in a somewhat awkwardly worded statement.

"Mr. Ackarman had left his car locked and it had been stolen by means of someone opening the no-draft window and then shorting the ignition system," stated Langdon in court.

After hot-wiring the car, Smith drove it back to Byng Avenue, then set about modifying it. Skey, who was still living at the bungalow despite his reservations about Smith, came home after work to find his pal in the garage working on the Galaxie, which he hadn't seen before. Smith had removed its front passenger seat, ostensibly to make the vehicle more accessible during a fast getaway. He had also attached a contact switch to the ignition. The contact switch would allow Smith to start the car more easily without a key.

Smith invited Skey to sit inside the Galaxie and check out his handiwork. Skey agreed, but first put socks over his hands so as not to leave fingerprints. With hands suitably insulated, Skey sat in the car and looked it over.

While eager to show off his car modifications, Smith wouldn't reveal when he planned to rob the CIBC bank. He only disclosed this information early Friday morning, July 24.

"I was on my way to work. It was reasonably early, about seven o'clock. I had to be at work at seven-thirty and he was still sleeping, and I was getting up. I got breakfast and I was leaving, and he came into the kitchen and told me that 'today' was the day," Skey testified.

Once again, Skey didn't report this conversation to police. On the witness stand, Skey said he was planning to spend the weekend at Bass Lake Provincial Park. He would be attending a religious retreat with his girlfriend and people from a youth group at the church he was attending. Skey was intending to head to Bass Lake once he finished his shift for the day.

Two other people were planning to pop by the Canadian Imperial Bank of Commerce at Bathurst Manor Plaza that day: Jack Blanc and his wife, Sally.

Blanc's extensive military records say he was born August 20, 1909, in Winnipeg. According to his son, the date is correct but not the location — Jack Blanc was really born and raised on a different continent.

The Blanc family "lived in what is now Ukraine, in what they called 'the Pale,'" recalls Stanley.

The "Pale of Settlement" was a special zone in the western part of Imperial Russia, where Jews were permitted to live — barely. Jewish residents had to put up with pogroms and prejudice on a regular basis. Morris Blanc — Stanley's grandfather — fled to Canada around the beginning of the First World War and moved to Winnipeg, with a view to bringing the rest of his family over. It took a few years, however, before his remaining family, including Jack Blanc, could make it out.

By the early 1920s, Ukraine had been subsumed by the Soviet Union, the world's first Communist regime. Jack Blanc might not have been eager to highlight this fact around conservative-minded military officials, speculates Stanley. This could explain why his father gave Winnipeg as his birthplace on most of his existing military forms. A Canadian Army document dated October 23, 1944, is one of the few reports that detail the Blanc family's true background.

While the form gets some details incorrect, such as Jack Blanc's place of birth, its contents generally corroborate Stanley's account of his family heritage: "Soldier born in Russia. He is of Hebrew faith. Father went to Canada in 1912. Mother followed with soldier ... Father was a tailor and furrier. Family in limited but adequate circumstances," states the document.

Jack Blanc entered school in Winnipeg. He dropped out after grade ten and became a furrier like his father. It would be his main occupation throughout his working life when he wasn't in the army.

On April 28, 1932, Blanc signed up with the Winnipeg Light Infantry Regiment, "starting a life-long association with the Canadian Army," as a subsequent courtroom document put it.

The regiment was a Non-Permanent Active Militia (NPAM) unit. The NPAM was a part-time military organization whose members trained in their off-hours. The same year Blanc joined he met a woman known as Sally (but named Sarah on military documents) at a Jewish community dance. A relationship ensued and the pair married on October 22, 1933. They moved from Winnipeg to Edmonton. Blanc again worked as a furrier and joined the reserve force of the Edmonton Regiment.

"He used to go a couple nights a week to [drill]. When the war broke out, he went right into it," said Sally Blanc in court.

The war in question was the Second World War, which began September 1, 1939, when Nazi Germany sent panzers rolling into

Poland. The fur-cutter signed up with the Canadian Army on September 4, before Canada officially declared war.

On his military forms, before, during, and after the Second World War, Blanc's name was given as "John Blank." It would eventually evolve into Jack Blanc (though still pronounced "Blank").

Blanc was made a sergeant, then shipped to Great Britain in late 1939 as part of the Edmonton Regiment. He was ordered back to Canada in March 1942 to instruct recruits at training bases.

Blanc returned to Britain in late September 1942 with the Essex Scottish Regiment. He served as a platoon sergeant in France and Belgium in 1944 and was hospitalized with burn injuries from an explosion.

Blanc earned several service medals for his steadfast conduct. Photographs taken of Blanc in uniform show a handsome serviceman with dark hair, a moustache, and a proud bearing. He also earned kudos from men who served with him, including Senator David Croll.

"He was a soldier's soldier. He was a perfectionist and an excellent soldier. Good sergeant major. He had a concern for his men [and] taught by example. He had a fine knowledge of firearms and [was] a man who had the confidence of the young boys," remembered Senator Croll in a *Toronto File* interview.

Shipped home in June 1945, Blanc took a job cutting fur for the Goldman Fur Company in Edmonton. He was a skilled worker who specialized in making mink coats and stoles, recalls his son. That said, Blanc was "hurt psychologically" by the war, remembers Stanley, who thinks he knows why.

In August 1942, when Blanc was safe at home instructing recruits, the Canadian Army spearheaded the disastrous Dieppe Raid. Canada's first major land battle in Occupied Europe was a bloody fiasco. Nearly a thousand Canadian soldiers died in a few hours of vicious combat.

Blanc had trained some of the troops involved — "young boys, seventeen, eighteen," says Stanley, and "he wasn't with them" when they were hurled against German defences on the coast of France. "Many of them were maimed, killed, or taken prisoner. I think this affected him for the rest of his life — that he survived, and they didn't."

Though traumatized, Blanc remained a dedicated soldier, who soon found a new war to fight.

After declaring independence in May 1948, the new nation of Israel found itself battling for its life against armies from neighbouring Arab countries. Israeli leaders pleaded for help and Blanc responded.

"By trade, Jack had been a furrier. But that was an accident of life. He was really a born military man who had missed his vocation. When Israel called for volunteers, Jack heeded the call and left to help the Jews create their homeland," stated Leo Heaps in a tribute to Blanc in the *Canadian Jewish News*.

Blanc was one of several hundred volunteers who sailed to Israel on a ship called the *Altalena* in June 1948.

"The *Altalena*'s passengers were men and women from all over Europe, Canada and the United States ... Jack Blank, a Canadian, was gun captain," noted a book called *The Secret Army*.

When the *Altalena* anchored off an Israeli beach, a shooting battle broke out between the Haganah (forerunners of the Israeli army) and the Irgun (a Jewish paramilitary outfit). Both groups were eager to claim the personnel and munitions on the ship for their own use. As gun captain, Blanc fired a few shots from the *Altalena* before abandoning the now burning ship.

"I first met Jack Blanc in Israel in 1948, when he and many volunteers jumped off the Irgun landing craft, the *Altalena*, on the beaches of Tel Aviv, amidst a fusillade of machine gun bullets. An abortive civil war was in progress between the Haganah and the Irgun, which fortunately did not last long," wrote Heaps.

Heaps said he "took one look at Jack and asked if he would like to join my small unit of the Israeli army in the Galilee. He promptly accepted the invitation, realizing he would have very little future in the Irgun," continued the article.

Blanc was "a seasoned soldier" who demonstrated "courage, forthrightness and loyalty," added Heaps.

"I would say he was the kind of soldier most anybody would like to have in their unit ... Acting as a sergeant in the Israeli army, he could handle his men well and certainly carry out orders as capable as anyone would want," echoed Israeli military colleague Leonard Fine on the *Toronto File* program.

Israel won its war of independence and, according to Stanley, his father was eager to stay and put down roots in the new nation. Arab countries had imposed a tight air, sea, and land blockade, however, and food in Israel was scarce. Back home in Canada, Sally Blanc, who was looking after the couple's young daughter, Diane, was informed of these developments.

"My mother was told you can go but don't bring your daughter. They're living on rationed food [in Israel] because there was a blockade. She wouldn't leave and my father wouldn't stay without my mother," states Stanley.

Blanc returned to Canada to be a fur-cutter again. Reunited, the Blancs had a second child, Stanley, who was born September 6, 1949.

Less than a year after Stanley arrived, the Korean War broke out and Blanc decided to join the fray. He re-enlisted in the Canadian Army in early 1952. An evaluation form written after Blanc passed an NCO (Non-Commissioned Officer) refresher course describes him as follows: "Very enthusiastic and cooperative, he performed his practical work fairly well. He has a tendency to rush things too quickly and to forget some of the basic principles of minor tactics."

Blanc was posted as an infantry platoon sergeant at a base in Ipperwash, Ontario, but problems emerged. Twice in December 1952, Blanc got drunk and acted up. On the first occasion he tossed a knife into the wall of the sergeants' quarters. On the second occasion he fired a pistol into the floor of the same quarters. He was sent to Westminster Hospital in London, Ontario, for a psychiatric evaluation, but the journey was interrupted. The jeep transporting him got into an accident, and Blanc suffered a fractured clavicle. He was apologetic about the intoxicated weapons incidents, but officials released him from the military.

On *Toronto File*, Fine was asked if Blanc "was a man who was unhappy when he was out of uniform?"

"I don't know if you could say unhappy, but I think the uniform did offer him certain things, whether you want to call it excitement or something you don't find in your normal humdrum life that the average person is involved with. I think basically he liked the army, and he liked the involvement with army life," Fine replied.

His army career behind him, Blanc took up work again as a fur-cutter. The Blanc family moved to North York, settling into the apartment on Wilmington Avenue. Blanc got a job with Schipper Fur Fashions, on Bay Street in downtown Toronto. Blanc swam at the Young Men's Hebrew Association (YMHA) in North York and led classes in scuba diving.

"He was tough on us, very tough. A tough personality — army-type tough. He made us work hard, but we loved it, because we wanted to learn … He put us through tough training, so we could learn to be good scuba divers. It was a very rough program. We were all lifeguards at the time," recalls Stan Lesk.

At some point in 1964, Jack and Sally decided a vacation would be in order. They also decided it would be a good idea to open a joint bank account, so they both could access funds while on holiday. Accordingly, before leaving on the vacation, the pair headed to their local CIBC branch, in the Bathurst Manor Plaza.

The Blancs entered the CIBC branch around 5:00 p.m. Jack Blanc sat down while his wife stood in line, waiting for an available teller. Then a rifle discharged, shocking everyone inside the bank.

"I just heard the shot … It was not just a little shot. It was a terrible combustion … I turned around and there was a man standing on the counter," testified Sally Blanc.

Initially, she thought the intruder resembled a clown, "but when you had another look at him, it looked a little more ugly — you know — really frightened you," she continued.

If Sally was frightened, her husband was furious — and he would soon be shot dead by the bank robber.

Roughly ninety minutes after Blanc was murdered, his body was transported to the coroner's building at Lombard Street and placed in the morgue. There, police searched through Blanc's clothing. From a shirt pocket, they removed a pack of cigarettes, matches, and an eyeglasses case. The pockets in his pants held coins, keys, Kleenex, and a wallet containing cash, a Canadian Army card, Social Insurance information, and a driver's licence. Blanc also wore a gold-coloured watch on his left wrist. Police placed this property in a bag, labelled it, then handed it over to Blanc's brother-in-law the following day.

After Blanc's clothing was thoroughly searched, Dr. Chester McLean performed an autopsy.

The pathologist wrote detailed notes about the post-mortem and later repeated some of this information in court. The pathologist described Blanc as five-foot four, weighing 145 pounds, and "well nourished but lean and muscular." During the autopsy, Dr. McLean removed multiple bullet fragments from Blanc's heart, lungs, and other body parts. There was massive damage to the army veteran's right thumb, internal organs, and head.

The bone at the base of Blanc's right thumb had been "completely shattered and the thumb was hanging by a few fragments of skin," testified Dr. McLean.

The "greater portion of the left ventricle and the right ventricle of the heart in the anterior portions — that's the forward portions — had been blown away, and in addition, portions of the pulmonary artery and portions of the aorta — the main vessels which lead from the heart — had also been blown away. This is a tremendous injury and would cause almost certain death," continued the pathologist on the witness stand.

This shot would have likely killed Blanc. Smith had fired again, however, and blew away half of Blanc's brain.

"The head wound was so massive that for any purpose the deceased was dead when that wound had been inflicted," stated the pathologist.

◆ ◆ ◆

That same evening, Skey returned to Byng Avenue after finishing his shift with Bowden Lumber. On the drive home, Skey heard reports about a bank robbery over the radio in his truck. The robber's identity was unknown. If Skey had an inkling that Smith was the perpetrator, he didn't mention his suspicions to police. Instead, once he got to the bungalow, he began packing for his church camping trip at Bass Lake Provincial Park.

The phone rang and Skey answered. It was Smith.

"Everything's all right. I will be home later," said Smith.

Skey thought little of this brief phone conversation. He continued his preparations for the religious retreat, then drove to pick up his girlfriend. Skey realized he forgot something — possibly his bathing suit and towel, so he returned to Byng Avenue.

Smith was home, hanging around the doorway that led to a pair of bedrooms.

"The accused was standing in the doorway, surrounded by money ... He mentioned to me that there was at least $20,000. I asked him what had happened, and he told me he had robbed a bank and when he was leaving apparently this man, Blanc, chased him out of the bank shouting that he was going to kill him, and the accused said that he, Mr. Blanc, had taken about three — I think it was two or three — shots at him," Skey told a courtroom.

According to Smith, it had been necessary to shoot Blanc; it was "kill or be killed," he told Skey.

Smith was calm as he related all of this to his roommate.

"He seemed pretty cool. He was not emotionally upset," testified Skey.

If anything, Smith was feeling generous. He knew Skey was going to Bass Lake, so he handed his friend $70 in small bills.

"Have a good weekend," said Smith.

For someone off to a religious retreat, Skey didn't seem unduly upset by his friend's confession. Skey left for his camping trip, with proceeds from the bloody CIBC robbery in his pocket.

◆ ◆ ◆

While Skey went camping and Smith contemplated his newfound wealth, accountant Carman Lamb went back to work shortly after the shooting. In 1964, employers didn't typically offer staff much in the way of support after traumatic events. Staff at the Bathurst Manor Plaza CIBC branch were expected to return to their duties, as if nothing had happened.

The shooting "was a Friday. I don't think we worked Saturday. We were all in the next working day. Except there was one gal who was fairly new. Her mother wouldn't let her back. But the rest of us all went back," states Lamb.

Army doctors then knew about Post-Traumatic Stress Disorder (PTSD), a common affliction among soldiers seared by combat, although they didn't refer to it by that name. Less well understood at the time was the fact civilians could also suffer from PTSD.

Lamb didn't think he had PTSD, however. He wasn't nervous about resuming his job but was concerned that the Beatle Bandit might pay a return visit.

"Where I lived, my parents had a mutual driveway. You had to walk down it to get in the side door when I went home. There were two garages and [a lot of] space in between and it was dark. If Smith had decided, 'I'm going to get you. You caused me a problem,' that would have been a perfect ambush spot. For a few nights, I was a little nervous about walking down my own parents' driveway," says Lamb.

Matthew Kerry Smith never took his revenge. Lamb did, however, receive the admiration of bank patrons who appreciated his courage the day of the robbery.

"The people there were really kind to me after [the holdup]. The clientele was quite kind. I was impressed how kind they were to me," he recalls.

Chapter Five

Portrait of a Hero

Three hundred mourners packed the Park Memorial Chapel on July 26 for Jack Blanc's funeral service. With Rabbi David Monson presiding, the service was attended by friends, family, and members of the General Wingate branch of the Royal Canadian Legion, which Blanc belonged to. Wingate president Allan Perly openly wept as laudatory tributes were heaped on the dead veteran.

Rabbi Monson, who was also a chaplain at the Wingate Canadian Legion branch, portrayed Blanc as a hero of the highest degree.

"To Jack Blanc, it was natural to stand up against gangsterism and hoodlumism, to fight to preserve law and order ... Unlike others, he naturally obeyed the Biblical injunction to be his brother's keeper," said Monson, according to the *Canadian Jewish News*.

After the service, dozens of vehicles travelled in a solemn procession to Mount Sinai Cemetery. When the cars passed the General Wingate branch headquarters on Bathurst Street, a Legion colour guard dipped its flags in Blanc's honour.

At the cemetery, thirty Legion members led by a kilt-clad piper escorted Blanc's coffin to the gravesite. An honour guard made up of members of the Queen's Own Rifles fired three volleys in the air. A trumpeter played "The Last Post" — a traditional funeral song for Commonwealth soldiers. Blanc's coffin was draped with both a Union Jack (Canada's new maple leaf flag hadn't been unveiled yet) and the Israeli flag. Legion members saluted, then tossed poppies on the coffin as it was lowered into the earth. Blanc's family looked on, devastated with grief.

The Canadian Legion set up a Jack Blanc Family Fund to raise money for his dependents. The stated goal was $25,000. A phone blitz was launched in tandem with in-person solicitation.

According to Perly, the $25,000 objective was quickly reached. In late September, Metropolitan Toronto Council agreed to provide Ms. Blanc with an additional $5,000 on top of this amount. While Metro Council voted unanimously on the matter, Alderman George Ben raised some contentious questions about Blanc's actions.

"The thing that troubles me, that we think it is alright if a man robs a bank or commits any other crime that we should seize a gun and go be judge and jury and executioner and shoot the man. So, I'm all in favour of compensating his widow because everyone should be looked after by society. But surely, we owe it to our own society to preserve law and order," stated Ben to his Metro Council colleagues.

In the face of harsh rebuttals, Ben stuck to his position, adding, "If a police officer shot a bank robber in the back, I'd say that he is guilty of murder. For that is not what his weapon is for. It is issued to him only for his own protection. So how can we condone when somebody else goes out with a gun and attempts to kill a citizen who is presumed innocent until proven guilty according to our system? I think it's incumbent on every one of us here to raise our voice on this point."

Alderman Ben would repeat this perspective during a September 28 broadcast of the CBC-TV news program *Toronto File*, which

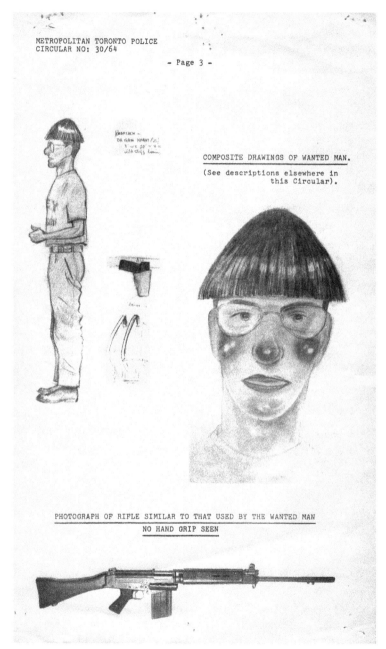

Wanted poster issued by Metropolitan Toronto Police, with an artistic (and inaccurate) depiction of the "Beatle Bandit."

also offered a clip of his remarks to Metro Council. The program, hosted by Ed McGibbon, questioned whether Blanc was a hero or a reckless vigilante. Sally Blanc was interviewed at length, looking blank-eyed and distraught. She spoke movingly about her husband and condemned the murderous actions of the Beatle Bandit.

◆ ◆ ◆

Finding Blanc's killer was a top priority for the Metropolitan Toronto Police. Drawings of the "Beatle Bandit," as he was dubbed, were displayed in newspapers and a seven-thousand-dollar reward was offered for information leading to his capture. Two thousand dollars of the reward money came from the Metropolitan Toronto Board of Police Commissioners with the remainder pledged by the Canadian Bankers Association.

Metropolitan Toronto Police issued an error-ridden circular asking for public assistance in tracking the killer down. Sketches in the circular made the bandit look like a circus clown with soup-bowl hair. The robber's disguise consisted of "a black, shiny, beetle-type wig. A rubber or plastic shiny, moulded face mask. This mask was flesh coloured with a red chin, red nose, and red cheeks. Yellow sunglass-type, glasses with metal rims. A white, short-sleeved T-shirt with the inscription, 'CKEY GOOD GUYS' printed across the front," stated the circular.

The suspect was described as "male, 25 to 30 years, 5'10 to 6', white, medium voice without accent" who "appeared to be Canadian." The circular even included a description of the guitar case Smith left behind in the bank. The case was described as "43 inches long; six inches deep; 16.5 inches at the widest point, five inches at the narrow end Blueish-grey imitation leather covering, with mottled effect. Dark blue cloth lining."

In addition to the guitar case, police hoped to uncover clues from the vehicles and weapons used in the holdup. The three cars involved in the robbery — the modified 1963 Ford Galaxie, the commandeered 1960 Pontiac, and PC Donald Jackson's shot-up police cruiser — were all taken to the No. 32 Police Station garage to be inspected.

The Ford Galaxie was photographed, then examined by mechanics and detectives. Police removed the faulty contact switch, then got in touch with Andrea Ackarman and invited him to check out his recovered vehicle. Ackarman looked the Galaxie over in the police garage, taking note of the missing front passenger seat. Glancing at the odometer, he said the car had been driven forty-six miles since he last saw it. He also thought there was a bullet hole in the left side of the car. In court, Deputy Crown Herbert Langdon also referenced a bullet mark on the Galaxie — an indication of Blanc's shooting abilities if true. The presence of a bullet hole was not firmly corroborated in police reports, however.

Smith's second getaway car had been located a day after the robbery. The Pontiac sedan was found in a grassy locale on Scott Drive near Yonge Street. The doors were unlocked.

After discovering the vehicle, police performed an initial inspection on the spot: "I made an examination of the interior of this automobile and during this examination, I found a paint-like substance which was pink in colour and this was adhering to the right side of the horn ring. I removed this pink paint-like substance and placed it in a container and sealed it," stated Detective Sergeant John Webster in court.

Police also photographed the car and checked for fingerprints. In the police garage, the Pontiac was subjected to a more thorough inspection. Investigators discovered what appeared to be two spent bullets in the car. By the time Smith had seized the Pontiac, Blanc was dead, and the only person firing was accountant Carman Lamb. Lamb never claimed to be a particularly good marksman, so the presence of bullets was an intriguing — if unconfirmed — discovery.

PC Jackson's shot-up police cruiser was also put under the microscope. Both front and back windows were shattered, and bullet fragments were found inside the vehicle. These fragments showed how close constable Jackson came to being killed when Smith fired at him.

As detectives pored over these cars, a parallel investigation was launched to track down the murder weapon. Nine shell casings from a rifle and eight casings from a pistol were recovered after the shootout. Analysis in a police lab determined that the pistol casings came from a Colt .45 semi-automatic handgun. Results were equally conclusive about the rifle casings.

"It was learned from examination of the expended rifle cartridge cases that the murder weapon was a FABRIQUE NATIONALE semi-automatic, 7.62 mm., 'Commercial' model. These rifles are manufactured in Belgium and distributed in Canada by the Browning Arms Company of Canada, Ltd., Montreal, Quebec," stated a detailed police report.

This report was written by Detective Sergeant Norman Hobson of the homicide squad. Det. Sgt. Hobson spearheaded efforts to track the rifle down and would prove to be a dogged investigator.

Hobson joined the force in 1949, working his way up to the homicide squad by the late 1950s. In June 1960 he travelled to the U.S. to take the FBI's gruelling twelve-week policing course. Hobson studied law, medicine, and various crime-solving techniques, and received a graduation diploma for his efforts.

Two years later, Hobson helped track down cop-killer Ronald Turpin and hitman Arthur Lucas. After both men were hanged at the Don Jail, Hobson escorted their bodies to the cemetery.

As police knew, the 7.62 FN rifle (described in Det. Sgt. Hobson's report as "the civilian model of the Canadian Army C-1 rifle") wasn't a common weapon outside of military circles. If the Beatle Bandit purchased the firearm from a legitimate dealer and not on the black market, police figured they might discover his name through sales records.

The RCMP asked Browning Arms for a list of FN rifles it shipped to Toronto-area dealers from 1961 onwards. When Browning Arms responded, it was discovered only two Toronto dealers carried the rifle: Hallam Sporting Goods at 621 Yonge Street and Modern Gun Shop on Danforth Avenue. Between them, these two stores had sold half-a-dozen FNs in recent years. Police decided to check in with these retailers first, in the hope of catching a lucky break.

Det. Sgt. Hobson visited Hallam Sporting Goods on the last day in July, looking for receipts. The store handed over sales slips from 1961 to mid-1964, which Hobson sorted back at police headquarters. It was not an easy task.

"Unfortunately for my purposes, every nut, bolt, screw, and firearm sold by Hallam's is recorded on a sales slip and these sales slips are not sorted into firearms and accessories and I had to go through every sales slip," stated Det. Sgt. Hobson in court.

After looking over countless receipts, Hobson determined that Hallam sold four FN rifles in the period he was examining. The receipts included the name and addresses of the buyers. Det. Sgt. Hobson tracked down three of the gun owners, all of whom confirmed their purchases. Hobson borrowed these rifles so they could be test-fired, and their shell casings compared to crime-scene casings. The weapons were test-fired at the Attorney General's Laboratory and none of the casings matched.

The fourth gun owner proved to be highly elusive. A sales slip stated that an FN rifle bearing serial number 2562 had been sold on January 10, 1964, to an "Owen Fox" residing at "19 West Ridge Drive." Some sleuthing revealed there was no West Ridge Drive anywhere in the Toronto area. There was a 19 West Ridge *Road* in Toronto, but when Hobson made inquiries, he learned the person living there was not named Owen Fox, nor did they own a rifle.

Hobson had come tantalizingly close to discovering the identity of the Beatle Bandit, only to be stymied by a phoney name and address on store paperwork. Of course, the detective didn't realize this at the time and plunged ahead with his investigation. When Det. Sgt. Hobson checked in at Modern Gun Shop, he discovered the store had sold two FNs between 1961 and mid-1964.

Hobson located the gun owners who had bought their weapons at this store. One of them lived in Scarborough, the other in Hamilton, Ontario. Test-firings were conducted again but no shell-case matches were found.

The persistent Det. Sgt. Hobson decided to expand his search. He asked the Browning Arms Company for a list of FN rifles it had shipped to dealers across the entire country for the past four years. Browning Arms was amenable to this request — provided the detective come to their head office in Montreal to examine the receipts himself. The company also said police would have to look through all its receipts to locate specific information about FN sales. In pre-email days, this information couldn't be sorted and sent electronically. Hobson flew to Montreal and visited the Browning Arms headquarters, in the company of an RCMP officer assigned to assist him. The pair left Browning Arms HQ with cartons filled with gun sale receipts.

"The Browning Arms Company keep a record of each individual firearm and the records are kept so that they have an invoice number sorted into various types of firearms which they sell," Det. Sgt. Hobson explained in court.

Working with the RCMP officer, Hobson determined that 205 FNs were shipped to dealers nationwide between 1961 and mid-1964. He also cited weapon serial numbers and gun retailer contact information for each purchase. Back in Toronto, Hobson and a police task force set about tracking down every rifle on the list.

"I wrote letters to various police departments throughout Canada and from these replies wrote further letters to police departments in Alaska, the State of Connecticut, Wisconsin, Minnesota, and New York City and requested these various police departments to contact the Browning dealers and search their records and find out who the guns had been sold to, contact the owners of these weapons and have them test-fired and submit fired casings to me. I supplied the various police departments with Attorney General seals and over the next several months I received many packages containing fired casings," Det. Sgt. Hobson explained in court.

Police traced all but sixteen of the rifles on Hobson's list. Some of the missing weapons were sold by a Winnipeg dealer who told police it would take too much effort to weed through paperwork to find information about his FN rifle sales.

Shell casings from rifles police did locate, or casings that were mailed to the task force, were examined by the diligent staff at the Attorney General's Laboratory. None matched the nine rifle casings from the crime scene. For all his work, Det. Sgt. Hobson had failed to crack the case.

As police tried to locate the murder weapon, a gun battle of a different sort broke out in the media. Following Blanc's murder, Toronto newspapers ran several pieces about the perceived laxity of Canadian gun laws. A blunt column in the July 28 *Telegram* stated: "Our gun laws are murder. Of all the grievances Canadians have against the Government for wavering before a pressure group, this is the most serious. That was proved once again last Friday on a crowded Downsview street when a citizen took on a holdup man — and lost."

The paper offered details about the weapon that killed Blanc and how it was likely purchased. The information was remarkably perceptive, given that authorities hadn't yet found the gun in question.

"Police believe the holdup man was using a semi-automatic or pump action .308 rifle purchased in one of Metro's many sporting good stores ... He required no permit proof of responsibility, competence honesty or anything else — except cash — to get it," fumed the *Telegram*.

As the *Tely* was aware, the Beatle Bandit had benefitted from a loophole in existing Canadian gun registration rules.

At the time, retailers had to file all copies of paperwork pertaining to firearm sales with a registry run by the RCMP.

While this system seemed strict, the registry excluded a variety of popular weapons, due to a peculiar definition of the term "firearm." Under the Criminal Code of Canada — the national legislation dealing with criminal offences and penalties — a firearm was defined as "a pistol, revolver or a firearm that is capable of firing bullets in rapid succession during one pressure of the trigger."

In other words, handguns and automatic weapons had to be registered while shotguns, bolt-action rifles, and semi-automatic rifles did not.

This wasn't a case of clueless legislators who didn't understand gun nomenclature and used a silly definition that excluded certain weapons from government scrutiny. Gun regulations had been tweaked in the early 1950s as part of an overhaul of the Criminal Code. House of Commons debates from that era make it clear that politicians knew exactly what the new measures entailed.

"Rightly or wrongly the definition of firearm includes — we are dealing now with the specialized definition — a revolver or pistol or automatic rifle," noted MP George Nowlan (PC — Annapolis-Kings, Nova Scotia) on June 25, 1951.

There was a logic, so to speak, behind these regulations. Automatic weapons were perceived to be particularly dangerous while "registration for hand guns is based on the idea that they can be easily concealed and thus useful to criminals," explained the *Telegram*.

Since criminals preferred pistols to long guns there was no need to register non-automatic rifles, said supporters of the new rules.

In conversations with police and colleagues, Smith never said he picked an FN because it didn't have to be registered. He might have chosen an FN simply because it was a highly regarded military rifle. If the rifle had had to be registered, however, it's entirely possible the store might have tried harder to confirm Smith's identity before selling him the weapon.

The gun registration loophole infuriated opinion-makers at the *Telegram*.

"If and when the rifle [used to kill Blanc] is recovered, police officers will know the frustration of trying to trace the owner of a murder weapon that should be registered — but isn't. It will be much like recovering a car involved in a hit-and-run accident, only to find it has no license plates and isn't registered with the Department of Transport," wrote a *Telegram* columnist.

The *Telegram* said long guns weren't included in the registry because Ottawa didn't want to offend hunters and target shooters, who made up a powerful constituency.

"Every time this issue is raised, there is a hue and cry from the sporting set — the hunters, the trap shooters, the woodsmen, the outdoor types. They regard the minor inconvenience of registering their weapons as an invasion of their private preserve ... Well, we've mollycoddled that lot for long enough," snapped the *Telegram*.

While the *Telegram* didn't offer data, Statistics Canada information gives evidence to the dangers of long guns. In 1964, there were ninety-one "firearm murder incidents," according to Statistics Canada. A little over 25 percent of these incidents involved handguns while nearly 70 percent involved rifles or shotguns (weapon type was unknown in some cases). Clearly, Smith wasn't the only killer to use a rifle that year.

The *Tely* proposed more restrictions on weapon transactions (no one with a criminal record should be allowed to buy a gun and penalties on sales to kids should be stiffened). The paper even suggested handguns might eventually be banned altogether.

"The authorities should withdraw immediately all pistols in civilian hands and prohibit their future sale and possession. This

will greatly increase the difficulties faced by criminals in the acqui-
sition of weapons," stated a July 28 *Telegram* column.

Once the death rate from gunshot wounds declines "as I'm
sure it will ... authorities should experiment for one year with an
unarmed police force," added the columnist.

These were provocative proposals, to put it mildly, particularly
a handgun ban (probably as much of a non-starter in 1964 as it
would be today). That said, Ottawa did get around to tighten-
ing gun regulations a few years after the Beatle Bandit's crime
spree.

Enacted in 1969, Bill C-150 prohibited gun sales to anyone with
a criminal record or an "unsound" mind. The bill also offered a
more sensible definition of what constituted a "firearm" (firearms
were now described as "any barrelled weapon from which any shot,
bullet or other missile can be discharged and that is capable of causing serious bodily injury or death to the person"). For the first time,
weapons were slotted into three different categories: nonrestricted,
restricted, and prohibited.

In the wake of Blanc's murder, the *Telegram* also criticized the
common practice of arming bank staff.

"Mr. Blanc might well be alive today if the bank manager had
not been issued with that pistol," wrote the paper.

This wasn't the first time the *Telegram* editorialized about this
same issue. The *Tely* had offered similar criticism following a previous robbery with strange echoes of Smith's rampage.

On May 19, 1955, Arthur Aronson and Lloyd Simpson stormed
into the Toronto-Dominion Bank at Dundas and McCaul Streets
in downtown Toronto. Armed with a sawed-off rifle and sawed-off
shotgun, the pair demanded money. Simpson entered the office of
bank manager William Davidson, shotgun in hand, and barked at
the man to step outside. With Aronson keeping watch on the staff
and two or three customers who were in the bank, Simpson rum-
maged through the teller's cage, grabbing cash.

The bank manager was not going to put up with this. Davidson tossed an inkwell through a plate-glass window to attract attention, then grabbed one of three .38 caliber revolvers the bank kept on hand. A wild melee ensued, with Davidson unloading five rounds at the robbers. At one point, Simpson dropped the shotgun, causing it to fire when it hit the floor.

Two people were shot during the gunplay, including Simpson, who was hit in the right shoulder. Simpson was arrested without struggle shortly after the robbery, as he lay in a rooming house bed, woozy from blood loss. Alan John Hannan, who was described in press coverage as either a bank messenger or a liabilities officer, was shot in the back and died.

"The fatal slug tore through the bank employee's shoulder, entered his lung, struck a bone and veered toward his heart, piercing the main artery, and lodging in the liver. He died within a few seconds," stated a rather anatomical write-up in the *Toronto Daily Star*.

Bank manager Davidson was so caught up in the gunfight he ran outside and tossed his empty pistol at the robbers' getaway vehicle. Aronson managed to escape but was tracked down and arrested May 28. The bloody robbery had netted a total of $2,300.

Aronson and Simpson were not charged with murder because Hannan was almost certainly hit by a shot fired by his own boss. Tests on the slug removed from Hannan's body indicated it didn't come from a rifle or a shotgun. The doctor who performed the autopsy couldn't confirm the round came from a .38 caliber revolver, but the evidence pointed that way.

Even Crown Prosecutor Henry Herbert Bull admitted as much at a preliminary hearing when he said the bullet in Hannan's body "could only have been fired by the manager," wrote the *Star* on June 30.

"Evidence at the inquest revealed that Mr. Davidson fired five shots at two gunmen ... and that his third shot struck Hannan in the back, killing him within minutes," echoed the *Globe* on November 10, in coverage of a coroner's inquest into the death.

During the inquest, it was revealed that although the Toronto-Dominion bank had three revolvers at the ready, staff weren't trained in how to use them. Lamb said much the same; despite the presence of two pistols in the bank, target practise was not mandated for staff at the Bathurst Manor CIBC branch.

The coroner's jury "recommended that all senior male employees of city banks be trained by police in the proper handling of firearms," wrote the *Globe*.

The idea that guns didn't belong in a bank was dismissed by Chief Coroner Alexander Lawson, who stated, "The banks must be armed, or else these cheap thugs will go into every bank in town. But the people in the banks must know how to use guns."

The *Telegram*, however, wondered if providing guns to bank staff was worth it:

> The question is whether an employee should use his gun to protect the bank's money and on this point the position of the bank authorities is ambiguous. They furnish the employee with weapons but instruct them not to resist as the money is covered by insurance. If the weapons are not to be used, why are they supplied? Should they be supplied in any case to men not trained to use them? If it were made known that the employees were unarmed and that there would be no resistance, would this not be an invitation to bandits? Are the guns supplied in case the gunmen fire first? These are among the questions that require study.

Stanley Blanc offers a similar opinion.

Bank revolvers "were just for protection only. It's not the Wild West of 1870. You're not supposed to go after a bank robber. [The bank money] is insured," says Stanley today.

Today, banks no longer stock revolvers and the FN rifle isn't available for civilian sale. An order-in-council issued December 23, 1982, under the Liberal government, classified the FN as a "restricted" weapon — making it more difficult to obtain and mandatory to register.

"The semi-automatic rifle of the design commonly known as the FN-FAL or Fabrique Nationale Fusil automatique léger, including any reproductions thereof or modifications thereto, is hereby declared, effective November 12, 1983, to be a restricted weapon," read the order-in-council, as published in the *Canada Gazette*.

Another order-in-council from November 29, 1994, added the FN-FAL to a list of prohibited weapons. Such firearms are reserved for police and military personnel only. Civilians who owned FNs could keep them if they were registered, but future sales were banned as of January 1, 1995.

While few people today think banks should stock revolvers, controversy over gun control still rages. There is currently intense debate in Canada about the merits of a long-gun registry. Many of the rifle registration arguments, pro and con, would have been familiar to newspaper readers in 1964, in the wake of the Beatle Bandit's rampage.

♦ ♦ ♦

The man who murdered Jack Blanc kept busy the rest of the summer and fall, banking money from the CIBC robbery, buying property, and enjoying a reunion with his girlfriend.

Eileen returned to Byng Avenue in early August following her extended visit out west. She brought her young daughter, Estelle, with her. Smith paid for Eileen's airfare and seemed fine with having a toddler in the house.

Smith did ask Eileen to do some chores, namely, depositing money for him at different banks. During the late summer, Eileen placed separate cheques worth hundreds of dollars or more into various accounts. Smith was upfront about the source of this money.

"He told me he robbed a bank," Eileen later told a courtroom.

Smith also told his partner he killed a man during the robbery and showed Eileen newspaper clippings to prove it. Eileen did not storm out upon realizing her boyfriend was a murderer. Maybe she felt trapped, with a small child to raise and no income of her own.

Richard Skey and Joe Bashutzky deposited thousands of dollars in cash and cheques for Smith as well.

Smith told Bashutzky to open accounts at Toronto-Dominion Bank and the Royal Bank of Canada. Bashutzky, who was working at Redpath Sugar at the time, followed these instructions. Once the accounts were set up, Smith handed over money from the bank robbery, which Bashutzky exchanged for different bills. It was a simple, but effective, form of money laundering that made it harder to trace any of the heist money to Smith.

As a reward for his labours, Smith let Bashutzky keep some of the money he was handling. Once again, Smith was completely open about where this cash came from.

"He said, 'I just robbed a bank.' Well, I thought he was just telling a joke, so I never paid too much attention to it at the time," Bashutzky later testified.

Smith was not known for his sense of humour. He admitted as much in interviews with police and psychiatrists. Bashutzky's comments could have been an attempt to put distance between himself and a criminal, or a rationalization for not turning in his friend. If taken at face value, his remarks suggests an odd lack of communication between Smith's pals. Had Bashutzky asked, Skey could have confirmed that Smith was indeed a bank robber. There is no indication Smith forbade his friends from talking to each other.

In addition to spreading cash from the CIBC robbery around, Smith purchased another property. His father was making money in real estate, so Smith decided to dabble in the same market. The plan was to earn rental income, to further advance the cause of revolution.

According to Skey, Smith looked at a few potential places before buying a fourplex apartment building on Elizabeth Street in Brampton, a city near Toronto. The total cost of the building was $60,000. Eileen and Skey were in on the deal, although almost all the money for the purchase came from Smith. Skey had a job at a drugstore at the time. Smith told him to write a cheque to a real-estate agent for a down payment on the building with an option to buy. Skey complied, and passed on a cheque, paid for with robbery money. Skey, who would write further cheques at Smith's behest for the Brampton property, pegged the total down payment at around $18,000. In addition to being point man for the purchase, Skey started a joint bank account with Smith in Brampton. This would allow future tenants to "pay rent directly to the bank," he testified.

While happy to participate in Smith's business ventures, Skey was having second thoughts about his living arrangements. Skey's personal relationship with Smith was becoming strained.

"I was fed up. I couldn't take it anymore. I couldn't understand him, and I was — I would say 'scared' because I am generally afraid of things I can't understand," Skey later told a courtroom.

By late summer, Smith was beginning to seriously frighten him. Skey worried about being shot by his gun-happy landlord.

"Hand-to-hand, I would not be afraid of him, but with the amount of guns that were in the house, there is no telling what he may do. He could pick up a gun and I might say the wrong thing and he could quite easily have shot me ... If he is unarmed and I am unarmed, I would not be afraid of him, but the other way around, in the house, if there is guns handy and he happens to get mad, there is no telling what he might do," Skey testified.

Skey got so anxious he was hospitalized in late August for what he described in court as "a nervous condition ... I was getting severe headaches, very painful, and they were too frequent, and the doctors thought it might possibly be a brain tumour and they tested for this and they didn't find anything, and they said they couldn't find anything physically wrong with me and suggested that I go to a psychiatric clinic."

Released after roughly two weeks in hospital, Skey moved out of Byng Avenue and into his own apartment. For all his wariness about Smith, Skey continued to drop by Byng Avenue on occasion to socialize. Also, Skey, Smith, and Eileen remained business partners in the Brampton property.

At some point in November 1964, Skey entered the Byng Avenue bungalow and immediately noticed a strange smell. Tracing the source of the stench, Skey ventured to the basement. He realized Smith was burning something in a laundry tub. The items being incinerated were strips of upholstery, taken from a car seat. The seat was from the 1963 Galaxie that had failed miserably as a getaway car. Smith had kept the car seat in his basement, amid other junk.

Eileen was apparently helping with the disposal of evidence, in contradiction to her own statements about being forbidden from entering the basement.

Skey was not impressed by what he saw.

"I told them not to burn the upholstery in the sink, because they are liable to burn the house down," said Skey in court.

Skey grabbed what remained of the car seat and placed it in a beer carton, along with some loose strands of upholstery. Smith took the metal frame of the car seat separately to a dump-site and threw it away.

Skey drove to an apartment building he had once worked at on a construction crew. The building had an incinerator, into which Skey dumped the beer carton and its contents. Though he no longer roomed with the Beatle Bandit, Skey remained a devoted helper.

Skey wasn't the only person in Smith's orbit going through a mental health crisis. On November 10 his sister, Lianne, brought their mother to see a medical expert. His name was Dr. Herbert

Hyland, and he was a former associate professor of medicine, specializing in neurology at the University of Toronto, and a hospital consultant. After retiring in 1950, Dr. Hyland, who was certified in psychology, opened a private practice.

Dr. Hyland first met Smith's mother in late May 1964. His initial encounter with Isabel Smith did not go well; she acted in a "somewhat antagonistic" and "very cold" manner, Dr. Hyland later testified. She didn't want to answer questions and abruptly ended the session.

"After a short interview, she got up and said, 'I'm leaving now' and she went. She wouldn't admit that she was in any way ill at that time or that she required any medical attention. She had discontinued a tranquilizing drug which had been formally prescribed and one thing I did manage to do I think, was to persuade her to go back on it again — taking it again," said Dr. Hyland in court.

Now, Isabel had returned to his office, and it was clear she was in worse shape than before. Isabel had stopped eating and bathing, said Lianne. She was convinced giant insects roamed her apartment and the only way to ward them off was to keep her appliances on all the time, including the stove. Other tenants in her building were petrified that she would burn the place down.

"She seemed much worse than when I had seen [her] previously. She talked volubly and showed greater variability to me. She was liable to become quite angry on occasions and other times, she would be smiling and relatively pleasant," testified Dr. Hyland.

Isabel had also developed some delusional conspiracy theories. She told the doctor that "Roman Catholics" were trying to force her to become a nun. These proselytizers were particularly aggressive; they accosted her in restaurants and yelled obscene remarks outside her apartment.

As far as Dr. Hyland was concerned, this persecution existed only in Isabel's mind. He concluded she was a paranoid schizophrenic and arranged the paperwork to have her committed to the Ontario Hospital, a psychiatric facility.

Isabel Smith's diagnosis was a long time in coming. Dr. Hyland would later testify that "the first evidence of this illness go back to about 1935, when she was about twenty-five."

This opinion would have been cold comfort to Isabel's twenty-four-year-old son, who was already terrified about going insane himself.

Chapter Six

One More Heist

Matthew Kerry Smith and his new friend Warren John Laidlaw sat in a 1949 Oldsmobile sedan, watching the street, and being watched in turn. The pair were in Sutton, Ontario, a village near the southeast shore of Lake Simcoe, scouting a bank for a possible heist. Smith was planning a new robbery, this time with a partner, which is why he brought Laidlaw with him on his journey to Sutton on November 23, 1964.

Smith, who had always worked alone, never explained why he decided to involve a second man for this robbery. The decision likely had something to do with his narrow escape after the Bathurst Manor Plaza heist. As a former military man, Smith knew a bit about strategy and probably figured he would be safer if he brought a wingman.

Laidlaw was a co-worker at the Dunlop plant. He was younger than Smith and married. The pair formed an acquaintance at work, and when Smith suggested a bank robbery, Laidlaw was receptive. It's possible that Laidlaw needed extra cash because he had a new wife and infant daughter to support.

Laidlaw's nuptials had taken place in March of that year. He was nineteen at the time of the marriage; his bride, Diane Judith

Price, was sixteen. Diane hailed from North Bay, Ontario, and worked as a typist. The same month the pair married, Diane gave birth to a daughter, named Peggy Sue.

Smith's target in Sutton was the local branch of the Bank of Nova Scotia. While the scouting mission was a wise idea, Smith didn't realize he was attracting attention. Only 1,470 people lived in Sutton, an hour from Toronto, and strangers tended to stand out.

Jack Tate, an assistant manager at a local hydroelectric station, noticed Smith's car prowling the streets of his community. He didn't recognize either man in the vehicle and thought they looked scruffy. The pair didn't seem like tourists out to sample Sutton's small-town charms. For one thing, they appeared unduly interested in the local police station.

In a big city like Toronto, two oddballs in a car might not be cause for alarm, but this was not a big city, and Tate was not someone who ignored fishy behaviour. He was in the habit of noting the licence plate numbers of vehicles that aroused his concern.

"I have always had this habit. But in this case, the car was travelling so slow that it was extremely noticeable. Perhaps if the car had been going faster, I wouldn't have bothered jotting the number down," Tate later explained.

Curiosity piqued, Tate took a pencil from a pocket and wrote "16924" — the licence plate number of the skulking vehicle — on a telephone pole. He later passed the number to Sutton police, who in turn passed it to other police stations. Tate wasn't quite as observant when it came to the make of the car. He told police the vehicle was a blue Chevrolet. Lawmen in nearby North Gwillimbury, another small community, were intrigued. Some outboard motors had been stolen recently from a local marina. Perhaps the mystery men in the Chevy were involved in that theft? North Gwillimbury cops kept the licence plate number on file for future reference.

Tate's sleuthing would have devastating consequences for Smith and his associates, but that was far down the road.

Three days before Smith went to Sutton on his scouting mission, a married couple called Wales placed an innocuous advertisement in a Toronto newspaper. The couple wanted to sell their eleven-year-old two-tone blue Meteor. According to their advert in the Cars for Sale column, they were asking $100.

A young woman who called herself Jackie Wilson contacted Ms. Wales. Jackie was interested in the Meteor and told the Waleses she wanted to see the car in person. Jackie travelled to their residence wearing "red high-heeled shoes, dark net stockings and a beige coat too thin to protect her from the biting cold," noted a 1966 *Toronto Daily Star* article.

Mr. Wales took Jackie for a test drive around the block in the Meteor. Following the test drive, Jackie entered the Wales home and was given a cup of coffee. As Jackie sipped her java, she told the Wales she lacked a driver's licence but wanted to buy the car as a surprise present for her boyfriend. The boyfriend was named Terry. Jackie said she lived on Johns Street in Scarborough, Ontario.

There was a slight problem; Jackie said she only had $90 on her. If the Wales could drive her to a nearby shopping plaza where Terry worked, she could borrow $10 from him and pay the balance on the car. Then, she would wait in the Meteor for Terry to finish his shift before surprising him with her purchase.

Jackie's proposal sounded reasonable, so Mr. Wales drove her to the shopping plaza while Ms. Wales followed in another car. Jackie got out, went into a store, then came back with $10. She combined this with the $90 she had with her and gave the Wales their asking price for the Meteor. The Wales gave her a receipt and asked her to sign an ownership transfer application.

"As it was a Saturday and the motor vehicle registration office was closed, she assured us she would get her vehicle permit first thing on Monday morning," Ms. Wales later explained in the *Toronto Daily Star*.

The Waleses took Jackie at her word, which turned out to be a bad move.

"In Ontario, and most other provinces, purchaser and vendor are equally responsible for transferring [vehicle] ownership within six days of transaction," Ms. Wales noted in the *Star*.

Until Jackie Wilson obtained a vehicle permit, the Meteor would remain registered in the name of Mr. Wales. Jackie kept the ownership transfer form and then stayed in the Meteor as the Waleses drove home in their other car.

That might have been the end of things, except that Jackie wasn't really named Jackie and the Meteor was going to be used as a getaway vehicle, not a present.

"The accomplice's wife, Mrs. Laidlaw, had purchased a car for $50, which was transported to the scene of the robbery," stated a subsequent Department of Justice memo.

The memo had the value of the sale wrong, but otherwise was accurate. Once Smith and company had the Meteor, it was taken to Sutton and left there. Specific details about who drove the car there and how they returned to Toronto remain unclear.

On November 27, Smith drove back to Sutton in his Oldsmobile with Laidlaw and a trailer towing a motorboat. Smith had purchased the motorboat specifically for the robbery. Smith steered his car and trailer to a spot on Lake Simcoe's western shore and parked.

A large body of water, with a surface area over 279 square miles (722 square kilometres), Lake Simcoe is popular with boaters and commercial fishermen. Smith had no interest in the lake's recreational attractions, however. After parking, he slipped the motorboat into the water. Once the boat was buoyant, Smith and Laidlaw climbed aboard, carrying concealed weapons. They hit the engine, scurried east across the water, and docked near Sutton. The men tied the boat up, then walked to where the Meteor had been parked previously. They drove the Meteor to the local police station, bursting in with pistols drawn around 5:30 p.m.

Sutton wasn't a high-crime area, which is why Constable William "Billy" Harris was the only lawman on duty that day. Harris was sixty-four and close to retirement. He looked up and saw a pair of strangers in red wool masks, dark glasses, blue jeans, and work boots, brandishing pistols. One of the intruders shouted, "This is a holdup!"

At first, Constable Harris thought it was a prank. Maybe someone was playing a preretirement practical joke on him? Harris brusquely told the masked duo to get lost. When neither man reacted, the constable realized this wasn't a prank. He reached for his service weapon, which was stored in a cupboard, not his holster. Before the constable could get his handgun, the strangers smacked him on the head. They pistol-whipped the veteran officer, striking him at least three times.

The now bloodied constable was handcuffed to the door of the jail cell in the station. The masked gunmen gagged their prisoner, then raced outside. The bandits seemed "extremely nervous and in a real hurry," Harris later told a local newspaper.

Smith and Laidlaw rushed to the Bank of Nova Scotia. They put away their pistols and burst inside the bank pointing "semi-automatic hunting rifles," wrote the *Globe and Mail*. The intruders aimed these weapons at staff and customers, amid much shouting.

To bank patron Harvey O'Neil, the two robbers seemed anxious and jittery. Laidlaw used the muzzle of his rifle to prod bank manager Gerald Goodwin. He wanted the man to move faster, but his rifle discharged — accidentally, he later insisted — and Goodwin was shot in the shoulder. The bullet passed through his flesh and struck bank clerk Brenda Taylor in the face. Taylor staggered, blood pouring from her jaw.

"Sorry, but these guns have a hair trigger," said one of the robbers.

Smith and Laidlaw were masked, so witnesses couldn't tell who uttered this apology. The words sound exactly like something

Smith would say, however. Following this remark, one of the robbers — again likely Smith given he was the leader of the operation — asked if anyone had first-aid experience. O'Neil said he did and was ordered to help Taylor. Upon examining the poor woman, O'Neil realized her wound was serious. He wasn't a doctor, so he asked permission to call one to treat the injured customer. The robbers were agreeable, so a call was placed for medical help. One of the gunmen kept asking out loud, "Is she going to die?"

While concerned about unintended casualties, Smith and Laidlaw had no intention of abandoning their mission. The pair seized handfuls of paper money from cash drawers and stuffed them into an army-style haversack. The bandits didn't order customers to empty their wallets and purses and hand over the contents — which made sense, given they seemed in a hurry.

Alerted by the gunfire and shouts from the bank, concerned citi-zens began flooding the Sutton police station with phone calls. These calls went unanswered, however, as Constable Harris was cuffed and helpless. Unable to get through, some residents called police stations in other nearby jurisdictions.

Margaret Veerdoole and her nineteen-year-old son, Derek, were ambling about Sutton when they heard the ruckus inside the Bank of Nova Scotia. Derek peeked through the window and observed a pair of masked gun men with rifles. He informed his mother, and she raced to a store to call Sutton police.

Smith and Laidlaw came storming out of the bank. Their exit proved as clumsy as their entrance. One of the pair dropped the haversack and paper money flew out over the sidewalk. As Derek watched in astonishment, the robbers frantically stuffed most of the cash back inside the bag, then ran off. Smith and Laidlaw climbed into the Meteor, drove to where they had left the motorboat, then ditched the car and sped west across the lake.

As Smith and Laidlaw made their getaway, Mrs. Veerdoole reappeared on the street. She informed her son that the Sutton police station wasn't responding to her frantic calls. Derek took off to investigate. The police station was locked, so he broke down the door. Inside, the boy discovered Constable Harris, bleeding and handcuffed. The quick-witted teen raced to a nearby service station and borrowed a set of heavy-duty wire clippers. Harris was freed and then taken to hospital, where he received twenty stiches in his head. Ambulances also picked up Goodwin and Taylor and took them to York County Hospital in Newmarket. Both survived, although Taylor required extensive surgery.

The pair responsible for this mayhem tossed their weapons into Lake Simcoe before reaching the opposite shore. They sank their boat in Shanty Bay, near the city of Barrie, then ran on foot to Smith's Oldsmobile. The pair got in and drove off.

While Ontario Provincial Police quickly established roadblocks around Sutton, they had no idea Smith and Laidlaw had switched cars. The OPP were looking for a "1953 or 1954 Meteor" noted the *Telegram*, and Smith and Laidlaw easily evaded capture in the Oldsmobile. When the pair counted their money, it came to roughly $10,500, worth about $90,000 today.

For all the clumsy aspects of the heist, from shooting two staff to dropping the loot, the operation was a huge success. Smith's plan had worked, and police were oblivious to the use of a motorboat in the getaway. It was arguably his best-thought-out robbery — and certainly the most inventive.

With his cut, Laidlaw took Diane to Texas. Smith went to Manitoba and got reacquainted with an old pal — Kenneth Amiotte. Amiotte was Eileen's brother. Smith first had met him in 1962, when the pair worked together at International Nickel. Amiotte had spent around three months at Inco, then returned home to Elphinstone. He was a couple of years younger than Smith, and the two men got along reasonably well.

Before he left Elphinstone, Smith asked Amiotte if he was interested in living with him in Toronto. Amiotte could take a bedroom at the Byng Avenue bungalow Smith occupied with his sister. Amiotte leapt at the chance.

"I was always getting into trouble in Manitoba … I wanted to get away from trouble in Manitoba … and I thought if I went someplace else, I would get a better start," Amiotte later explained in court.

Flush with cash from the Sutton robbery, Smith paid for Amiotte and his girlfriend, Iris Houle, to fly back with him to Toronto. Amiotte and Iris both took up residence at Byng Avenue.

While happy to accept Smith's largesse, Amiotte realized quickly that his benefactor was a tad eccentric. For a start, Smith liked to brag about his various criminal exploits. Amiotte thought these remarks were a bit odd but didn't take them seriously, he claimed.

"He used to joke to me about this and that, and I never believed him because he was always a 'joker' to me. He always joked to me," said Amiotte in court.

Like other colleagues who testified about Smith, it's likely Amiotte wanted to put distance between himself and his former friend. Amiotte's sister knew Smith wasn't joking when he talked about robbing banks. If Amiotte did realize Smith wasn't kidding, it didn't stop him from hanging out at Byng Avenue or motivate him to call police.

A few days before Christmas, Matt Smith decided to put aside his differences with his son and pay a visit to the expanded household at Byng Avenue. Smith Senior had been unhappy with his boy for some time. The incident with the stolen car had been bad enough, but then Smith compounded his situation by walking away from therapy.

For all that, the holidays were approaching, and Smith seemed to have settled down, even without psychiatric intervention. He was working hard at Dunlop Tire, had a new girlfriend, and now owned a house.

Matt Smith bought a little tray and apron set as a Christmas gift for toddler Estelle, then drove to Byng Avenue. Smith greeted his father and let him inside. Matt Smith looked around and noticed a group of people he didn't recognize, glued to the television set. Smith introduced his father, to muted response.

"I came in there and [my son] said, 'Hi, folks. I'd like you all to meet my Dad.' Nobody looked up. Everybody kept on watching television," Matt Smith recalled.

Smith Senior tried to put on a happy face. He stayed for a time, but the visit left him depressed and disturbed. Beyond Eileen and Estelle, he wasn't sure who most of the people were in his son's house. He was upset to discover that Smith had quit his job at Dunlop Tire and wondered how he was earning a living.

Matt Smith wasn't the only person connected to the Beatle Bandit who was having a miserable holiday season. The Waleses were beginning to regret ever putting their vehicle up for sale.

Media coverage of the Sutton robbery consistently mentioned that a blue 1953 or 1954 Meteor was seen speeding away from the bank, the bandits at the wheel. The car, which was soon recovered by police, was still registered to Mr. Wales.

At first, the Waleses tried to convince themselves that any similarity between the car they sold to Jackie Wilson and the getaway vehicle was just a coincidence. Their concern deepened when Ms. Wales tried and failed to find a listing for Jackie Wilson residing on Johns Street in a Toronto-area phone directory. Ms. Wales looked at a map and discovered there was no Johns Street in Scarborough, either.

Concern turned to panic when detectives showed up at the Waleses' home, asking pointed questions. What connection did the couple have to the Sutton robbery, demanded police.

Several tense interviews ensued. Authorities finally concluded the Waleses had unwittingly sold the getaway vehicle and were not involved in the heist. Changing tack, Toronto detectives showed the Waleses mug shots of young women, to see if they recognized "Jackie Wilson" among their ranks. The couple couldn't spot her, and police moved on to pursue other leads. The Waleses contemplated their ordeal, and how close they had come to being swept up in a police dragnet.

If tracking down the owner of the blue Meteor proved fruitless, police were about to catch a lucky break with a different vehicle. The licence plate number and description of the suspicious vehicle citizen Tate spotted in Sutton had been passed to Metropolitan Toronto Police. Toronto detectives checked around and discovered that the car with plate number 16924 was registered to Matthew Kerry Smith, living at 31 Glenforest Road in Toronto.

Detectives visited this address to see if Smith knew anything about an outboard motor theft near Sutton. Smith's mother answered the door and curtly explained that her boy no longer lived there. Isabel Smith wouldn't say what his current address was and seemed baffled when police asked about her son's Chevrolet. She brusquely informed the detectives that her boy drove an Oldsmobile then dismissed them from her doorstep.

Unfriendly as she was, Isabel had provided police with a valuable bit of information. They now knew the precise make of the car Matthew Kerry Smith drove, in addition to his licence plate number. Plate number 16924 was added to the Metropolitan Toronto Police list of cars to watch for.

◆ ◆ ◆

At 11:15 p.m., on the evening of Wednesday, January 6, 1965, Police Constable Robert Greig went on duty at Station No. 53, near Yonge Street and Montgomery Avenue in north Toronto. Toronto doesn't usually get the kind of bitterly cold winters that afflict cities such as Winnipeg, Montreal, and Ottawa. Still, temperatures were below the freezing mark as Greig's shift began. As a member of the motorcycle squad, the constable didn't have the luxury of patrolling in a heated squad car.

PC Greig was assigned to patrol an area east of Yonge Street to Bayview Avenue, and from Mount Pleasant Cemetery to Lawrence Avenue East. Fully exposed to the elements, the policeman left Station No. 53 at roughly 11:30 p.m.

Greig steered his police-issue motorcycle south on Yonge Street. He went past Eglinton Avenue, a major east-west roadway, then parked in a service station near Yonge and Davisville Avenue. There, he began eyeballing vehicles, taking note of their licence plate numbers. PC Greig checked these against the police auto list, which featured dozens of licence plate numbers printed neatly on a paper form. Some plate numbers had symbols next to them, indicating a wanted vehicle or a car whose owner had an outstanding warrant. In a few cases, plate numbers had been given a special mark warning officers to be cautious when approaching the vehicle.

Within a few minutes, Greig spotted a blue 1949 Oldsmobile sedan, licence number 16924, travelling north up Yonge Street. He observed two male occupants inside the car. PC Greig consulted the auto list, and the plate number was on it. The car wasn't cited as stolen, but the fact it was on the auto list was enough for PC Greig. The constable started his motorcycle and followed behind the Oldsmobile. As he rode, the dexterous policeman radioed in the licence plate number to a dispatcher, asking for information about the car.

As the Oldsmobile approached Eglinton Avenue, the constable noticed a police scout car parked on the east side of Yonge Street. The yellow scout car was facing north. PC Greig took one hand off his motorcycle grip and motioned to get the attention of the constable inside the scout car. Greig pointed at the Oldsmobile, indicating he required assistance. At the wheel of the scout car, PC William Roberts got the message and started his engine. He followed behind Greig.

The Oldsmobile passed Eglinton Avenue and proceeded a few blocks north. Just before Castlefield Avenue, constable Greig made his move. He revved his motorcycle and raced in front of the Oldsmobile, signalling to the driver to pull over.

Up Yonge Street, near Erskine Avenue, PC Klaus Hubner was conducting a foot patrol. He glanced down the roadway and saw a motorcycle cop trying to pull over an Oldsmobile. The driver of the Olds seemed to be ignoring the signal to stop, so PC Hubner stepped off the sidewalk and onto the street. The constable, formerly of the West Berlin police force, faced the oncoming Oldsmobile with his palm held out. It was an unmistakable order to stop. The car jolted to a halt in front of PC Hubner.

Greig appraised Hubner of the situation, then asked him to check the car out. PC Hubner strolled to the driver's side of the Oldsmobile. The window was rolled down and the constable asked to see the driver's licence, ownership permit, and proof of insurance.

"What seems to be the trouble? Is this a spot check?" asked Matthew Kerry Smith, from the passenger seat.

"No. I have no idea. It could be pretty well anything. This car is wanted," replied PC Hubner.

As Hubner talked to Smith, the radio dispatcher got back to PC Greig, who was sitting on his parked motorcycle. The dispatcher said the Oldsmobile's plate number matched a car connected to the theft of some outboard motors in cottage country. Detectives from the break-and-enter squad were interested in speaking to the occupants of the vehicle. PC Roberts, who had parked nearby, approached Greig and asked if everything was alright. The constable assured him it was so Roberts hung back, ready to help if needed.

Another police vehicle joined the scene. Police Sergeant Ernest Gibson drove up and parked his cruiser, then conferred with Greig. A decision was made to take the Oldsmobile to Station No. 53, so the driver and passenger could be questioned about the outboard motor thefts. PC Hubner was asked to sit in the back seat of the Olds so the driver wouldn't take off.

Hubner sat in the back, then checked the licence given to him by the driver. The licence identified the driver as Kenneth L. Amiotte, born February 20, 1942, and living at 213 Byng Avenue in Willowdale. PC Hubner asked again for ownership papers and proof of insurance.

"I own the car," said Smith.

Smith took an ownership permit from his wallet and gave it to the policeman. The permit listed his mother's address at 31 Glenforest Road. PC Hubner asked Smith if this was where he lived.

"No. I live at 213 Byng Avenue in Willowdale," Smith replied.

"How long have you been living there?"

"Two days," said Smith.

As Hubner continued to examine his papers, Smith asked, "What seems to be the trouble?"

The constable in the back seat said he had no idea.

"How come this car is on the wanted list?" asked Smith.

PC Hubner didn't answer and soon the car was on the move. Sergeant Gibson halted traffic so PC Greig could lead a procession of vehicles south to Police Station No. 53 at 2398 Yonge Street. Greig motioned for the Olds to follow.

Amiotte made a U-turn and followed the motorcycle cop. Police Sergeant Gibson and PC Roberts drove behind Greig, in their respective cars.

The Oldsmobile and its escorts arrived at the police garage just after midnight. The car stopped near the rear garage doors on Montgomery Avenue. Smith exited the car and Greig walked behind him into the garage. Police Sergeant Gibson ordered the Olds to proceed into the garage. PC Roberts stayed outside in his scout car, watching the two men enter the station. PS Gibson left the scene, after receiving a call about a fire.

Amiotte drove inside the garage, then stepped out of the vehicle upon Hubner's order. Amiotte was told to pop open the car trunk so police could conduct a search. Then, the two suspects were taken into the station.

Standing before the Sergeant's desk, Smith and Amiotte were instructed to empty their pockets and place the contents on a counter. Police immediately noticed that Smith had blood-stained money in his wallet. Before they could ask why he was carrying bloody cash, a dark, metal object fell from the back of Smith's belt and onto the floor. PC Greig, who was searching Amiotte, was startled when he saw what was lying on the floor near Smith's shoes.

"He's got a gun!" shouted a constable.

A policeman darted forward and snatched a small, black Browning 6.35 mm pistol off the floor.

A constable demanded to know if the gun was loaded.

"No," lied Smith.

The pistol was examined. There was a round in the breech and five in the clip. The Browning might have gone off upon impact with the floor. Constables eyed the pair warily. According to the *Star* and the *Telegram*, a further search revealed that Amiotte was also armed, with a rifle hidden in his pants leg. That weapon was also confiscated.

Amiotte was told to sit in a chair in the southeast corner of the room while Smith was seated next to a teletype machine. The men were positioned so they weren't facing each other.

Police ordered Smith to be quiet, but he continued to gab. PS Gibson returned to the station around 12:30 a.m., January 7, after receiving an update about developments inside. Gibson spoke with Smith, who treated him to a monologue about the morality of brute force. Smith said he was fine with violence, provided no kids were involved. Violence between men or between a man and a woman was permissible in his view, but he drew the line at child abuse.

PS Gibson recounted some of Smith's comments in court. Smith expressed admiration for Nazis, Southern U.S. racists, and "parts of the Communist Party. He didn't agree with the Russian Communists, but he admired the Chinese Communists because they apparently were getting somewhere with violence," testified Gibson.

During his discourse, Smith never offered any opinions about fascist or Communist ideology. His interest in extremist groups hinged on their willingness to use violence to further their goals, not the content of their doctrines. Smith was motivated by a vague notion of revolutionary struggle and didn't have much of an actual political agenda.

Smith also touched on his personal life. He said his father was rich, his mother was "crazy," and that Canadians should have the same legal rights to gun ownership as their American counterparts.

When asked by detectives why he happened to be carrying blood-stained money, Smith stated that he might have "rolled a drunk for some of the money," stated a subsequent *Toronto Daily Star* article. In other words, he was suggesting he mugged someone and in the process the victim's money was splattered with blood.

Smith was arrested for possessing an offensive weapon. After receiving a police caution, Smith muttered that he might have grabbed the pistol from the same person he allegedly mugged.

It was a strange alibi, but things were about to get even weirder. Detectives Brian Albright and Robert Dougall escorted Amiotte back to Byng Avenue to look around. At this point, police thought they were merely dealing with a potential motorboat engine thief who had a pistol and some oddball opinions.

The inside of the bungalow was dark when Amiotte and the two detectives arrived around 2:00 a.m. An outside porch light was on and Amiotte used a key to open the front door. Detectives entered and the four occupants—Eileen, Estelle, Iris Houle, and Laura

Bone — awoke. Laura Bone was Eileen's cousin, who happened to be staying at the house.

More police arrived and a detailed search commenced. A Fabrique Nationale (FN) semi-automatic .308 rifle, serial number G2562, was found in a basement closet. The weapon was loaded with a full magazine and a cartridge in the breech. Cops also located the titanium bulletproof vest Smith had fashioned, a rifle handgrip daubed in pink paint, and many, many guns.

Detectives had spent months trying to track down an FN rifle with the serial number 2562, in connection with Jack Blanc's murder. It started to dawn on authorities that Smith might be the elusive Beatle Bandit.

Police removed twenty-two weapons from the Byng Avenue bungalow, including rifles, pistols, and airguns, and hundreds of rounds of ammunition. Officers were startled at how haphazardly the weapons were stored. Guns — many of them loaded — were found in closets, under beds, and in other obvious spots. It was an incredibly dangerous environment for anyone living in the bungalow, particularly Eileen's little daughter who wasn't even three years old at the time. Today, Estelle says she knew where all the guns were, but was wise enough, even at her young age, to leave them alone.

Detectives Dougall and Albright took some of these firearms, then placed them in the back seat of their car, after making sure they were unloaded. They returned to Station No. 53 and fetched Smith, to take him downtown to Metropolitan Toronto Police headquarters. The latter was housed in the former head office building of Imperial Oil at 92 King Street East.

It was 6:15 a.m. on the morning of January 7.

The detectives told Smith to sit in the front, between them. There wasn't room in the back, and the detectives wanted to keep Smith away from his guns, despite the fact he was in cuffs and the weapons lacked bullets.

As Det. Albright drove, Smith glanced over his shoulder to gaze at his confiscated firearms. "It looks like I'm in real trouble," he said. Pause, then, "I've got enough trouble here to last me a lifetime."

These were the opening notes of another long monologue.

"On the way down in the car the accused Smith continued to talk, and he said that he wanted to do something important with his life. He didn't want to be just an ordinary worker. He said his crimes were not for selfish reasons, but to get finances to use, along with force, and his guns, to change the government," Det. Albright later testified in court.

"He said violence was the only way to bring about a change in the government which would be good. Violence would tend to break down the morale of the people and make them used to violence and then, when a group of men — and it wouldn't have to be a large group — started to overthrow the government, the people would join in. He said he didn't think he really would do it, but he would like to," continued the detective.

Abruptly, Smith dropped his revolutionary rhetoric to propose a challenge.

"How would you two like to get a medal shooting me for attempting to escape? Give me one of those guns — just a handgun — and you each take rifles and we will get out and fight it out," he suggested.

To Smith's disappointment, neither detective expressed interest in fighting a duel.

"He then said that he thought we were yellow and felt that we were cowards," Det. Dougall later testified.

Det. Albright parked the car at headquarters around 6:30 a.m. Still in cuffs, Smith was escorted to a seventh-floor room. He was handcuffed to a chair, then Det. Albright departed for a few minutes, leaving the prisoner in the company of Det. Dougall. When Det. Albright returned, he began asking Smith about his background. Smith gave his name, address, level of education, and the names of family members. Det. Dougall and Smith both smoked as this information was compiled.

"Well, I guess the next thing is to take me and photograph me and fingerprint me, I guess I'll be inside for a long time. I don't want to be in this position ever, but I'm not afraid," said Smith.

Smith began to talk, as Det. Albright wrote down every word.

"I only wanted to do something significant with my life. I believe if you are going to do something you should do it well. You're a good policeman. You know your job and I know mine. I might have been a policeman but I'm on the other side. I made quite a bit of money, but I'm not taking any trips to South America. I'm not too greedy. I just like to live fairly good and not have to worry about bills coming in all the time like the workers. You probably think I'm crazy, but money isn't the only reason. I really would like to overthrow the government. People blame the government, but it is not the government that's at fault. The people are soft, and the government gets sloppy. Then someone comes along and changes it and if they are successful, instead of being criminals, they are the government," said Smith.

Smith punctuated this rant with long pauses. He offered some self-reflection, noting, "The only way is force. I really believe you could overthrow the government by force, and I would like to do it. I was doing all right, but I made mistakes. You got a break tonight, but I wasn't so smart, I kept the guns. Now I'm in real trouble but I'm not afraid. I don't care what happens. I'd rather live good for a short time then plod along doing nothing until I am sixty or seventy. If it's over now — I've lived pretty good."

During a pause, Det. Albright finally managed to ask a question.

"What do you think is going to happen to you?" inquired the detective.

"You know what's going to happen to me," Smith replied, making a hanging gesture around his neck.

On the witness stand, Det. Albright was asked if Smith was joking about revolution and violence. "No. He appeared to be quite serious about the whole thing," replied the detective.

At some point, Det. Dougall left the interrogation room to transport Smith's confiscated weapons into the station. The detective carried the guns from the back of his police car into an office on the seventh floor. During the transfer process, Det. Dougall encountered Detective Sergeant Norman Hobson, who was starting his shift. Hobson had spearheaded the fruitless effort to track down the rifle used to kill Blanc. Now, police were reasonably certain they had the gun and its owner in custody. Det. Dougall directed Hobson to the room where he had placed Smith's confiscated weapons and invited him to look them over.

In court testimony and written reports, Det. Sgt. Hobson didn't offer any insights about his feelings that morning. It must have been deeply gratifying, however, to see his prey cornered.

A little before eight, Det. Sgt. Hobson inspected the FN rifle removed from Byng Avenue. The detective noticed something odd; while one part of the rifle had the serial number 2562, the gun grip and some other parts were marked with serial number 1550. The latter was the serial number of a rifle from Winnipeg that Hobson hadn't been able to trace. It seemed Smith had purchased two FNs — one from Hallam Sporting Goods, the other from a Winnipeg dealer. Smith had swapped parts between weapons (a rifle breech block with the serial number 2562 was found at Byng Avenue in a suitcase with Smith's name on it).

In court, Hobson couldn't explain why Smith had switched the gun grips. It is possible Smith was trying to make it more difficult to track down the rifle. A clever move, if true, given the extreme difficulty police faced trying to find the murder weapon.

Det. Sgt. Hobson also examined a Colt .45 caliber semi-automatic pistol and a homemade titanium bulletproof shield retrieved from 213 Byng Avenue. With another detective in tow,

Det. Sgt. Hobson entered the office where Smith was being held and got his first look at the suspect. Smith was uncuffed from the chair and escorted to Room 718, an unpretentious space with a bookcase, filing cabinet, desk, and five chairs.

Hobson left the room, to contact the Attorney General's Laboratory. A lab representative arrived at police headquarters and collected the two FN rifles, .45 Colt pistol, and other items confiscated from Byng Avenue. The guns would be test-fired, to see if the shell casings matched cartridge casings from the crime scene. The serial numbers on the blood-stained cash from Smith's wallet were also scrutinized. They matched the serial numbers of money from the vault at the Bank of Nova Scotia in Sutton.

Once the transfer was complete, Det. Sgt. Hobson returned to Room 718 at roughly 9:50 a.m. Sitting before a typewriter, Hobson gleaned further background information from Smith. Once this was done, the detective cautioned Smith on a murder charge. It was a few minutes after 10:00 a.m.

"Matthew Kerry Smith, you are arrested on a charge of murder. Do you wish to say anything in answer to this charge? You are not obliged to say anything unless you wish to do so, but whatever you say will be taken down in writing and may be given in evidence … Do you understand the charge of murder and the caution which I have just read to you?" said Hobson.

"Yes, I do," replied Smith, as the detective typed his response.

"On July 24, 1964, the Canadian Imperial Bank of Commerce, 221 Willington Avenue, was held up and robbed and a customer shot and killed. What if anything, do you wish to tell me about this?" asked Det. Hobson.

"There is a lot to say," said Smith.

And then Smith went silent for half a minute. He requested that Hobson stop typing and then gave further instructions.

"You ask the questions, and I will answer by nodding my head," said Smith.

It was an unorthodox way to proceed, but Det. Sgt. Hobson was game. He re-cautioned Smith, then asked again if he understood the nature of the charge against him. Smith nodded.

The detective repeated the background details about the Bathurst Manor Plaza CIBC holdup, then asked, "Did you rob that bank and shoot Jack Blanc?"

Smith nodded his head twice.

There was further discussion, then detectives took Smith to the ground floor where he was fingerprinted and photographed. Smith was returned to Room 718 and the interrogation continued. Smith began rambling about extremism and violent revolution once again.

"These references were not said in a jocular fashion. He appeared to be serious about what he was saying," noted Hobson, in court.

Police sent out for food around 12:40 p.m. Smith was given a fried-egg sandwich and a coffee. After finishing his food, Smith asked if could phone Eileen. Permission was granted. Hobson explained how to make an outside call on the police phone, and Smith got Eileen on the line. He spoke quietly — the only words police could make out were "are you alright?" and "sorry." When Smith was done, police resumed questioning him.

While he was one of the Beatle Bandit's most determined foes, Hobson acknowledged that Smith seemed genuinely concerned about Eileen, his partner.

"He spoke of his love for his wife — referring to his common-law wife," Hobson later testified.

That same day, Eileen, who was now pregnant, was arrested at Byng Avenue. Detectives cautioned two other women in the house — Iris Houle and Laura Bone — but didn't arrest them. Joe Bashutzky was located by detectives from the holdup squad and taken into custody.

On the afternoon of January 7, police also rounded up Richard Skey, who did not go peacefully. When three detectives arrived at

Skey's Avenue Road apartment, they discovered he wasn't home. A bathroom window was jimmied open, and a detective was hoisted inside. Once in the apartment, this officer unlocked the door for his colleagues.

Upon his return, Skey was not pleased to find a trio of lawmen in his apartment. A "stiff fight" ensued and Skey was overpowered, wrote the *Star*. His place was searched, and police located a .25 caliber semi-automatic pistol, a .38 semi-automatic pistol, a Winchester .30-30 rifle, and some ammunition. Skey would eventually face a charge of possessing an unregistered handgun.

Taken under guard to police headquarters, Skey had a chance encounter with Smith, who was being taken back to Station No. 53. It was a little before 5:00 p.m.

"We took [Smith] to the washroom and, on coming back out of the washroom, Detective Gilbert and Detective Cameron were just getting off the elevator on the seventh floor and they had in custody a man I now know as Richard Skey," Det. Sgt. Hobson later stated in court.

Smith and Skey passed each other in the hallway, but "there was no sign of recognition passed between the accused and Skey and we returned to room 718 to get our belongings," added Hobson.

Eileen, Amiotte, Skey, and Bashutsky would all be charged with being accessories after the fact to murder.

"This little-used charge is laid against anyone believed to have received, comforted or assisted a criminal and has a maximum penalty of 14 years," explained the *Telegram*.

If Smith showed no interest in Skey's fate, he remained deeply concerned about Eileen. As he was escorted back to Room 718, he asked, "Has my wife been arrested too?"

"Yes. She is on her way down here now," replied Det. Sgt. Hobson.

"Well, I better tell you about it now," said Smith.

Instead of taking Smith to Station No. 53, police asked him to sit down in Room 718 again and the interrogation continued.

Smith began speaking at length about the CIBC robbery and Blanc's murder. He allowed Det. Sgt. Hobson to type up his comments. Smith paused frequently, gathering his thoughts as the detective repeated some of his earlier questions.

When Smith described his actions in the CIBC branch, he added a few touches of bravado into the account.

"I ordered all the men out of the bank also. I said, 'If anyone wants to search for a gun, I'll take you on. If you're man enough. I doubt it,'" said Smith.

Given that no one reported hearing him say anything of the kind, the statement smacked of macho revisionism.

In a similar vein Smith praised Blanc and dismissed accountant Carman Lamb's shooting abilities.

"I assumed when [Blanc] started shooting bullets so close to me, compared to the teller who I knew instinctively was missing widely, I thought he had been staked out in the bank as a policeman or a professional gunman and I didn't want to end up another Peterson … Jack Blanc was a very brave man but never the less, I killed him. Although I killed him, I always respected the bravest man I ever fought," said Smith.

Peterson was a Toronto-area bank robber who had been shot and left severely disabled. Smith seemed to fear this outcome more than the possibility of being killed. Smith's dismissal of Lamb's marksmanship was ironic, given that what might have been two of Lamb's spent bullets were recovered from the commandeered Pontiac, according to police reports.

During his interrogation, Smith took full responsibility for his own actions, stating, "I am the only one who can be condemned for this crime."

Some of the questions posed to Smith were technical in nature. Part of his police interview reads as follows:

Det. Sgt. Hobson: What kind of rifle was it that you carried?
Smith: I carried a Fabrique Nationale .308.
Det. Sgt. Hobson: What kind of a pistol was it that you carried?
Smith: My trusty .45. Later this didn't prove to be quite so accurate, but then my rifle shots were not quite where I aimed them.
Det. Sgt. Hobson: How much money did you obtain?
Smith: $25,000.
Det. Sgt. Hobson: Do you wish to tell me what happened to this money?
Smith: I spent it. That's all.
Det. Sgt. Hobson: Is there anything else you would like to say?
Smith: What else can I say?

When the confession concluded, Smith was asked to read his statement over, then sign it. Smith offered a few minor corrections, then applied his signature, as did Det. Sgt. Hobson and another officer, serving as a witness. Smith asked for a cigarette and was told to help himself from a pack on the table.

◆ ◆ ◆

At some point that day, Smith rested in a cell. The police and press weren't quite so relaxed. At an afternoon press conference, Metropolitan Toronto Police Chief James Mackey was downright exuberant. He described the Beatle Bandit investigation as "the biggest case in the history of the Metro force."

Toronto newspapers splashed the story across their front pages.

"Found in a Byng Avenue home during today's investigation was an arsenal which included 14 rifles, eight handguns, a crossbow, and an armour-plated vest," stated the *Toronto Daily Star*.

Police said, "two of the guns were FNC-1 semi-automatic rifles which fire either 7.62 mm military ammunition or .308 soft-point hunting ammunition used for hunting North American big game," noted the *Globe*.

Around 9:20 p.m. on January 7, Smith was taken back to Police Station No. 53, where he was booked. That same evening, his father drove home from work, oblivious to the day's developments. Matt Smith stopped along the way to buy a newspaper, which he tossed on the front passenger seat of his car, planning to read it at home. At a red light, Smith Senior glanced at the front page. The main headline caught his attention.

Oh. They've got the Beatle Bandit, said Matt Smith to himself.

He looked over the opening lines of the article, then froze in shock when he came to the name of the suspect in custody. The Bandit was his son.

Matt Smith pulled over. He sat in his car for hours, alternating between tears, memories, and plans.

"The conviction that he had often had that his son was insane came flowing back over him," wrote Scott Young, in the *Globe*.

After debating what to do, Matt Smith pulled himself together. For years to come, he would mourn the loss of his child to madness and the victims his boy left in his wake. But at that moment, there were matters that required his immediate attention. Matt Smith returned home, placed a call to his company lawyer for advice, and tried to think of ways to help his sad, sick son.

Chapter Seven

Jailed, Analyzed, Condemned

Around 9:30 a.m. on January 8, 1965, detectives drove the Beatle Bandit from Police Station No. 53 to magistrate's court in downtown Toronto. The temperature that morning was slightly above freezing, rising a couple degrees by noon with a bit of cold rain — typical Toronto weather for early January.

Smith was in a talkative mood during the ride, his captors later reported in court. Among other topics, Smith discussed the contact switch he had installed in the Bathurst Manor Plaza getaway car.

"The accused stated that he had used a blue drill to make the holes for the switch in the car. The switch was bought at Yonge and Steeles — he didn't remember where he bought the cap from — the cap that was left in the stolen Galaxie — and that he had bought the CKEY shirt on Yonge Street north of Dundas," testified Detective James Read.

Smith's monologue ended when the detectives arrived at City Hall, where the magistrate's courts were located. Finished in 1899, the old City Hall was an imposing Romanesque-style building featuring a tall clock tower and a central entrance graced by triple arches. Later in 1965, a new city hall designed with futuristic flourishes would open, with great fanfare, just down Queen Street.

Smith was hustled into a heavily guarded courtroom where he faced Magistrate Donald Graham. The justice read the charges against Smith, which now included murder and two bank robberies (the Bathurst Manor Plaza heist and the Christmas Eve, 1963, holdup of the Toronto-Dominion Bank).

When asked, Smith said he understood the nature of the charges against him, then was remanded and led away.

As Smith ruminated in a jail cell, the Toronto press went wild with the story of his capture. A photograph on the front page of the *Star* showed a detective holding Smith's homemade bulletproof vest. The *Telegram* described Constable Robert Greig as an "eagle-eyed officer" and ran a picture of him receiving "a hero's welcome from his wife" in the form of a kiss.

PC Greig would also be honoured with a CKEY Radio "Good Guys Good Citizen Award." The award form praised Greig for his "keen observation and persistent action in trailing a stolen car, leading to the arrest of two hold-up men and possible murder[ers]."

While Kenneth Amiotte was not a killer, the comment underscored the intense media focus on the Beatle Bandit and his associates. The *Star* published pictures of Amiotte, Eileen, Joe Bashutzky, and Richard Skey being taken into custody, all of them blocking their faces from view with hands or clothes. A more flattering photograph of Eileen (described as "murder suspect Matthew Smith's common law wife") holding Estelle appeared in the *Telegram*.

Other articles recounted Blanc's death and the CIBC robbery. Newspapers were also intrigued by the huge weapons cache found at Byng Avenue ("Arsenal Seized; Man, 24, Charged in Beatle Killing," read a front-page headline in the *Globe and Mail*).

The bungalow continued to be of great interest to Toronto police, who returned several times to search the place. On January

11, detectives confiscated tools, gun magazines, and books with titles such as *How to Be a Crack Shot* from Smith's abode. They also uncovered bank books and financial papers dealing with the Brampton fourplex purchase.

Smith bided his time at Toronto's Don Jail, a miserable stone structure on the east side of the city, awaiting the results of a preliminary hearing. The hearing would establish if there was sufficient evidence to proceed with a criminal trial.

During January and February, Smith was examined in prison by Dr. Ronald Stokes (the same psychiatrist who had diagnosed him as schizophrenic in 1961) and Dr. Harry Hutchison, chief psychologist at Toronto Psychiatric Hospital. Dr. Hutchison, who was also a clinical teacher in the University of Toronto Faculty of Medicine, gave Smith an IQ test, and had him fill out the Minnesota Multiphasic Personality Inventory (a commonly used personality test).

Later, Smith would also be scrutinized by Dr. Michael Tuchtie, head of the Forensic In-Patient Unit at Toronto Psychiatric Hospital and Dr. Norman Easton, a psychiatrist at the Ontario Hospital in New Toronto.

If Smith's case made it to criminal trial, the conclusions of these medical men would be used to gauge his state of mind during his rampage.

Meanwhile, the wheels of the justice system continued to turn. A now contrite Richard Skey appeared as a Crown witness at the preliminary hearing, which began February 11. He was given protection under the Canada Evidence Act, which meant he could testify without facing new charges based on what he said in court — provided he told the truth. Like any witness, Skey would face a perjury charge if he lied in court.

With Chief Magistrate Arthur Klein presiding, Skey discussed how he had disposed of the Galaxie car seat and bits of Smith's disguise. Skey admitted he deposited money for Smith and participated in his real-estate venture.

"Skey said he took part in the purchase of an apartment building in Brampton, which was bought in his name and Smith's and Miss Griffiths', with a down payment of about $18,000 in cash. He said Smith negotiated the purchase of the apartment building," wrote the *Globe*.

The preliminary hearing clarified details about Smith's costume. Previous media mentions said Smith wore a clown mask or makeup during the Bathurst Manor Plaza holdup. Newspaper illustrations perpetuated this falsehood by making the Beatle Bandit look like a circus performer. In fact, "[Smith] wore a Beatle style wig pulled over a mask which resembled French President Charles de Gaulle," stated the *Globe*.

Policemen, bank officials, and Eileen all testified at the preliminary hearing as Smith watched and listened. The *Globe* described him as a "tall, dark-haired, bespectacled man, dressed conservatively in a three-piece grey suit with an oversized striped dress shirt that hung limply around his thin neck."

When the hearing concluded February 12, the court committed Smith to stand trial for capital murder. Evidently, the justice system thought he was sane enough to be tried in court — though an insanity defence might still save him from conviction. Otherwise, his chances were irredeemably bleak.

Historically, Canadian courts had shown little mercy to people convicted of serious offences like murder. From the time of Canada's semi-independence until the early 1960s, anyone convicted of murder automatically received a death sentence. Such sentences could be commuted, but for the most part politicians and the public were content to see harsh justice done. A total of 710 people were executed in this period, all by hanging.

A change to the Criminal Code in 1961 created a distinction between capital and non-capital murder. Killing a police officer or prison warden, or killing someone in a planned, deliberate fashion or in "the course of certain crimes of violence," as the tweaked

Criminal Code put it, was considered capital murder. Anything else was considered non-capital murder.

A conviction for non-capital murder meant life in prison, at worst. Capital murder was still punishable by hanging, however, and death sentences were still being carried out. Convicted murderers Ronald Turpin and Arthur Lucas, for example, were hanged together at the Don Jail on December 11, 1962.

The Beatle Bandit was now fighting for his life.

◆ ◆ ◆

Skey continued to provide helpful assistance to police. Shortly after the preliminary hearing ended, detectives met him at his Avenue Road residence.

To prepare Skey for his role as a Crown witness at Smith's criminal trial, police decided to test his memory. They took him to the Bathurst Manor Plaza and asked Skey what he recalled about the place from his previous visit with Smith.

"At the preliminary trial they showed me a picture of the bank and I couldn't recognize it from the picture … [Detectives] picked me up one morning and they drove me around and this is when I recognized the bank," Skey told a courtroom.

Memory primed, Skey would offer revealing testimony in court against his former friend.

Regina v Matthew Kerry Smith — as Smith's criminal trial was officially titled — opened Monday, May 10, in Ontario Superior Court in Toronto before a jury of nine men and three women. The prosecution was led by Deputy Crown Attorney Herbert Langdon, while Smith's counsel was John O'Driscoll, the same lawyer who had represented him at the preliminary hearing.

O'Driscoll had previously handled the appeal of Steven Truscott, a fourteen-year-old boy in small-town Clinton, Ontario, sentenced to hang for murdering a classmate in 1959. His role in the case is recounted in the harrowing book *"Until You Are Dead"* (O'Driscoll is described as "a senior and well-respected lawyer"). O'Driscoll would go on to successfully defend rock star Jimi Hendrix after he was arrested on drug charges in Toronto in 1969.

A complex figure, O'Driscoll expressed misgivings about birth control and divorce (contentious issues at the time) in an essay he wrote for the 1965 book *Brief to the Bishops: Catholic Laymen Speak Their Minds*.

During his later career, O'Driscoll served as a controversial judge. Some of his rulings and remarks were criticized, and he was accused of "consistently favouring the Crown," wrote the *Globe and Mail*.

For now, however, O'Driscoll was single-mindedly focused on keeping his client from being convicted and hanged.

Inside the courtroom, the capital murder charge was read out loud, and Smith pleaded not guilty. Once this formality was done, Justice William D. Parker laid out some legal fundamentals for the jury. Jurors were told to keep an open mind and closely follow the evidence. The trial might be interrupted by the occasional "voir dire" — a debate between lawyers about the admissibility of certain evidence. Jurors would be excluded during such discussions. Housed in a hotel in their off-hours, the jury was ordered not to talk about courtroom testimony with outsiders.

In his opening remarks, Langdon mapped out the crime scene, then walked jurors through the events of July 24, 1964. He didn't skimp on details or colour.

"Having emptied his .45 caliber pistol, the bandit then opened fire on Blanc with his rifle which he was still carrying. One shot struck Blanc in the hand and continued on into his heart. The second shot removed a large portion of the back of Blanc's head. Blanc, of course, was killed instantly," said the Deputy Crown.

Langdon mentioned some of the physical evidence he would be introducing, including shell casings and weapons. The list of courtroom exhibits would eventually fill several pages in the trial transcripts. In addition to physical evidence, "there will be approximately fifty-five witnesses called by the prosecution," added Langdon.

Smith, for his part, "showed a keen interest in the selection of the jury and the Crown's opening statement ... When the first juror was being selected, Smith remarked, 'He seems all right to me.' From then on, he remained silent," reported the *Telegram*.

Detective Harold Coon of the Metropolitan Toronto Police Identification Bureau was among the first to testify. The detective, who photographed the crime scene, described the chaos he observed at Bathurst Manor Plaza.

If Det. Coon was dry and factual, Sally Blanc offered high courtroom drama on the first day of the trial. Dressed in black, with a shawl on her head, Sally described her husband as a "very military minded" man who became enraged when no one would stand up to Smith.

Angry as he was, Blanc was a reluctant vigilante, insisted his wife. She claimed accountant Carman Lamb egged him on, even darting back into the bank to fetch him a pistol.

"I said, 'Please don't do it. Don't do this because my husband will be killed,' I said, 'Don't give him a gun. Please' and he didn't listen to me. Never answered me never even looked at me," testified Sally Blanc.

She spoke of the awful moment Blanc was shot dead and said Smith was "cursing like anything" during his murderous rampage.

Given the jury's natural sympathy for a widow, O'Driscoll trod lightly during cross-examination.

"Now, you have told us about Mr. Lamb giving your husband this gun. I take it from what you have said that it was pretty well all Mr. Lamb's idea. Is that right?" he asked.

"That's right," replied Ms. Blanc.

"Your husband did not really want to have any part of it?"

"Well, I don't know about any 'part of it.' He was just very upset the police hadn't arrived and he just didn't want this man to get away. This is the type of person he was. He was very much for discipline, as you can see," said Sally Blanc.

Other witnesses depicted Blanc as a hothead who instigated the deadly shootout and said Smith was calm throughout the melee.

"I went into the bank to get the gun, and on the way back out, Mr. Blanc came in. I was going out the first set of doors ... he got the gun from me," testified Carman Lamb, who was now working for the Guaranty Trust Company.

On the stand, Lamb explained how he was the person responsible for loading the bank revolvers with only four cartridges. This was to prevent accidental discharge, he said. The deputy Crown attorney was primarily interested in his interactions with Blanc.

"Do you know whose idea this was that Blanc should get your revolver?" asked Langdon.

"Oh, it was his own," replied Lamb.

"Did you offer it to Blanc?"

"Oh, no, sir. No, definitely not."

Liquor store manager Harry Caesar corroborated this account. A police report noted that Caesar "is of the Hebrew faith and is required, by his religion, to cover his head with a skull cap when taking his oath." The fact Toronto authorities felt it necessary to explain this gives a sense of the parochial attitudes of the era. With head properly covered, Caesar said Blanc wrestled the pistol from Lamb.

"Mr. Blanc started to run, and I ran beside him and tried to tell him not to use the gun but throw it away and let someone else try to catch him because I thought he would get killed," testified Caesar on May 10.

Salesman Hartley Lepofsky said much the same.

"When we were out in the parking lot, Mr. Blanc was building himself up, yelling, 'Let's go after him. There's enough of us to take him. There's only one of them. Why should we let him get away?' and this continued, with him building his courage," testified Lepofsky.

Far from being a voice of reason, Sally Blanc, "encouraged the issue by saying that he was a crack shot, and someone get him a gun," he added.

The second day of the trial featured a voir dire session. The jury was told to return to their hotel as opposing counsel argued. At stake was the testimony of thirteen witnesses, mostly police constables and detectives. These witnesses took the stand, then the judge decided what testimony could be repeated before the jury. For a variety of reasons, some statements were not allowed to be placed into evidence. Once the voir dire ended, the jury was recalled.

Detectives who were permitted to testify spoke about the weapons confiscated at Byng Avenue and Smith's remarks in custody praising violence, Nazis, and Communists.

Smith's courtroom behaviour continued to attract the attention of the press: "At times he raises his foot to the seat and lounges on his knee and other times turns around as though looking for a familiar face among the spectators ... Smith is a good looking, lanky man and is neatly dressed in a dark suit and vest and wears horn-rimmed glasses," reported the *Telegram*.

A heavily pregnant Eileen testified under the protection of the Canada Evidence Act. Speaking in a quiet voice, she was repeatedly admonished by Langdon to speak up. Her testimony included the following exchange:

Langdon: Now, did you ever receive any money from Smith?
Eileen: Yes.
Q. Now what did you do with this money?
A. Put it in the bank in the National Trust.
Q. And why did you do that?
A. Put it in there because he told me to put it in a bank.

Q. Now before you received this money from Smith, did you have a bank account anywhere?

A. No.

Q. Did you have to open an account?

A. Yes.

The subject of Smith's real-estate transactions came up:

Q. Who bought this apartment in Brampton?

A. Matthew Smith and Richard Skey and I.

Q. Well, did you put any money of your own into it?

A. Yes.

Q. You did?

A. No.

Q. Well, did you have any money or not?

A. No.

Q. All the money you got you got from whom?

A. Matthew Smith.

Skey, also granted protection under the Canada Evidence Act, testified May 14. He repeated his remarks from the preliminary hearing and tried to defend his inaction despite knowing Smith's plans. He said he didn't tell police Smith was going to rob the CIBC branch at Bathurst Manor because he was both loyal and fearful of his friend.

"While Skey testified, Smith sat restlessly in the dock. During much of the trial yesterday, Smith removed his shoes and sat in his stocking feet," noted the *Globe*.

Detective Sergeant Norman Hobson testified about the extensive search for the murder weapon. On the stand, Hobson offered a detailed account of the interview he conducted with Smith at police headquarters and read his confession into the record. This testimony revealed Smith's admiration for Blanc (newspapers seized on his remark about Blanc being "the bravest man I ever fought").

Vaclav Krcma, a ballistics expert from the Ontario Attorney General's Laboratory, offered technical testimony. Krcma compared seven rifle cartridge casings taken from the crime scene with casings he produced by personally test-firing an FN with the breech bolt and breech bolt slide found at the Byng Avenue bungalow.

"As a result of my microscopical comparison I came to the conclusion that all seven exhibits which I have just named were beyond any shadow of doubt fired by Exhibit 48, breech bolt, serial number 2562 and breech bolt slide, serial number 2562," Krcma testified.

In other words, the .308 FN semi-automatic rifle bearing the serial number 2562 owned by Smith was the murder weapon. Krcma also said crime-scene pistol shell casings matched casings produced by test-firing Smith's confiscated .45 caliber Colt semi-automatic.

When O'Driscoll launched his defence on May 17, he didn't deny that his client killed Blanc. What mattered was Smith's mental state at the time he committed the murder, he insisted.

"To put it in a word, the defence in this case is insanity and I submit to you ladies and gentlemen of the jury that the evidence I propose to call will substantiate that defence," said O'Driscoll.

It was a long shot defence strategy, but not entirely futile. Of the 199 Canadian adults and juveniles charged with murder in 1965, a total of 10 were "acquitted for insanity" according to Statistics Canada. Bleak odds, but given the overwhelming physical evidence and eyewitness testimony, an insanity defence was O'Driscoll's only real hope.

Canadian criminal law has always followed a British legal principle called the M'Naghten Rule (or M'Naghten Test). Established in the 1840s, the Rule centres on a simple question: Does a defendant charged with a crime understand the nature of their actions?

In other words, do they realize they did something wrong. If the answer is yes then they are considered legally sane and can be subjected to a trial. On the other hand, a suspect who is so mentally befogged they don't grasp the implications of what they did is considered legally insane. And being insane — in a legal, if not a medical sense — can be grounds for acquittal.

Canada's first Criminal Code, from 1892, put things rather bluntly: "No person shall be convicted of an offence by reason of an act done or omitted by him when labouring under natural imbecility or disease of the mind, to such an extent as to render him incapable of appreciating the nature and quality of the act or omission and of knowing that such act or omission was wrong."

This principle remained a fixture in the Criminal Code, even as its content was revised and condescending language edited out: "No person shall be convicted of an offence in respect of an act or omission on his part while he was insane," stated Section 16 of the Criminal Code at the time of Smith's arrest.

The insanity defence was not a get-out-of-jail-free card, however. If an insanity defence was raised, the Crown was almost certain to challenge it. Which is why so many experts were called to probe Smith's psyche. Both the Crown and Smith's defence team wanted to establish if he was truly mentally ill.

Regardless of the outcome of his trial, it was unlikely Smith would walk free from the courtroom. A murderer acquitted on the grounds of insanity in the 1960s could expect to be involuntarily committed until authorities deemed him or her ready to rejoin society. The end result could be a lifetime of confinement in a mental hospital. Better than jail, but hardly freedom.

As the first defence expert to testify, Dr. Herbert Hyland spoke about Smith's mother, whom he had examined the year before.

"I came to the conclusion that she was a long-standing case of schizophrenia, of paranoid type ... I certified her to the Ontario Hospital. I made out the papers," stated Dr. Hyland.

Having established that mental illness ran in Smith's family, O'Driscoll called Dr. Harry Hutchison to the stand. Dr. Hutchison said the test he administered to Smith indicated he had an IQ of 109, "in the high average to bright normal range."

While intelligent, Smith suffered "from a serious form of mental disorder known as paranoid schizophrenia," he added.

Dr. Hutchison said he arrived at this conclusion based on the results of tests he administered to Smith and comments he made during his jailhouse interviews.

"Mr. Smith drew an analogy of robbing banks to a surgeon performing an operation; if someone is killed, it is like the failure of an operation with one difference — the man who robs the bank stands to die, while the surgeon does not," stated the witness.

Dr. Hutchison continued, "He felt that robbing banks was a method for raising money and to create an ever-widening circle of violence which would cause people to become concerned about the government and which would result eventually in the violent overthrow of the government ... He also said that people who rob banks were interested in getting money whereas he was mainly interested in combat training."

For all this, Smith could be perfectly coherent, even reasonable at times, said the doctor. Smith complained about the lack of funding for psychiatric services in Canada, for example. He was also annoyed that the federal government ignored the concerns of young people (a position plenty of Canadians would have agreed with in the 1960s).

During cross-examination, Langdon repeatedly suggested that Smith had been wrongly diagnosed and was really a psychopath. Psychopaths lack warmth, empathy, and emotion, but their thinking process is generally intact, which is why they can be extremely effective predators.

Wouldn't someone with schizophrenia be too stupefied to perform the advance planning necessary to rob a bank, demanded the deputy Crown.

Dr. Hutchison said no. Like most people with schizophrenia, Smith had moments of clarity.

"I thought he showed ability to plan. There were some minor instances of woolliness in his thinking, but, by and large, I did not consider that he had a disorder or thought which made it impossible for him to plan," said the witness.

Considerably more is known about schizophrenia today, but the defence experts at Smith's trial were quite familiar with the condition. In the face of repeated questions about misdiagnosis, doctors tried to explain there are different types of schizophrenia and different levels of impairment. Someone with schizophrenia could be plagued with debilitating hallucinations one day, then able to function reasonably well the next.

For all that, Langdon did have a point. While the press tended to focus on the more eccentric elements of Smith's heists (shouting "Merry Christmas!" and wearing a Beatle wig, for example), his robberies demonstrated a high degree of cunning and preplanning. Smith took care to wear disguises and source getaway cars, for example. The Sutton robbery involved a great deal of prep work and centred on a clever ruse (taking a motorboat across Lake Simcoe and using a second getaway car). The Sutton heist did feature some unplanned elements, including the accidental shooting of two bank staff and dropping the loot on the sidewalk. Still, Smith and Warren John Laidlaw had managed to escape with a large sum and evade capture.

The question at hand, however, was not whether Smith was accurately diagnosed but if he was insane under the law. When Langdon asked if the defendant knew right from wrong, Dr. Hutchison started talking about crimes Smith hadn't been charged with. Judge Parker said another voir dire was in order and told the jury to leave the courtroom. When the issue was resolved, the justice called the jury back.

Next on the stand was Dr. Ronald Stokes, who said he had changed his opinion of Smith after talking to him in prison. In

1961, Dr. Stokes had concluded that Smith was schizophrenic but didn't pose a danger. The doctor still believed Smith suffered from schizophrenia, citing as evidence his delusional goals about revolution and tangential thinking process (in conversation, Smith would often leap from topic to topic, with little obvious segue, and make nonsensical points). If anything, his schizophrenia was more pronounced than it had been in the early 1960s, said the doctor. He was also convinced Smith had become dangerous.

"His attitude toward courageous behaviour makes him almost like a kamikaze pilot of World War Two. He has nothing to lose. He is prepared to take chances that other people — other people such as criminals I have examined who are not mentally ill — would never think of taking," stated Dr. Stokes.

Smith's "abnormal thinking coupled with his relatively high intelligence" gave him "the capacity to plan in a devious and cunning manner," he added.

Dr. Stokes offered some insights about mental illness and heredity.

"If you take 1,000 people, the number of schizophrenics one would expect to find would be approximately eight," he said.

"That is 0.8 percent?" asked O'Driscoll.

"Point eight percent. And if one parent suffers from schizophrenia, the ratio jumps up to 14.4 percent. In other words, 14.4 per one hundred, and if both parents suffer from schizophrenia, this figure jumps to 39.6 percent … so we do feel heredity plays a very definite role," explained Dr. Stokes.

The doctor was quick to add that researchers didn't believe schizophrenia was directly inheritable from parents, but resulted from multiple factors, genetics being one of them. Experts today might debate the accuracy of these percentages, but the point stood: schizophrenia had a strong familial component.

Cross-examination fell into a repetitive pattern. Langdon would cite one of Smith's achievements, such as modifying his getaway car, then ask if this showed rational thinking. Dr. Stokes wouldn't budge; Smith might be rational at times but was still schizophrenic, he insisted. The doctor also proved to be an excellent foil for the deputy Crown.

"Did [Smith] ever try to organize a group and overthrow the government?" demanded Langdon.

"He did not, and very few do with this type of thought disorder. Many people believe they are direct descendants of the English throne, but few of them go over to Buckingham Palace and claim their right," replied the doctor.

> **Q.** Do you think there is anything inherently insane about a son who wishes to prove himself in the eyes of his father?
> **A.** Oh no, not in that way.
> **Q.** I imagine quite a lot of quite normal sons feel that way?
> **A.** Oh yes, but they don't usually rob a bank to do it.

Trying to recover from this fumble, Langdon demanded, "Are you saying anyone who robs a bank is insane?"

"No, sir. I would suspect their motives though, if they robbed a bank to prove to their father that they were as good as they were. I would be seriously questioning it," said Dr. Stokes.

"Did Smith know it was wrong to rob banks?" demanded Langdon.

"He knew it was legally not permitted but he felt that it was morally right."

"He also knew that it was wrong did he not, to shoot people?" continued the deputy Crown.

"He knew that it was not legally permitted but if, in the course of his original pursuit of his aim someone was killed, then he felt it was morally right and justified," responded Dr. Stokes.

There were more questions from the deputy Crown, then Judge Parker announced a break for the day. When testimony resumed on

May 18, Dr. Stokes took the stand again. In response to Langdon's questioning, the doctor said he believed Smith was fit to stand trial, even though he was schizophrenic. Dr. Stokes underscored the difference between the legal and medical definition of mental illness.

"A man can be very sick — very mentally ill — quite psychotic — and still be fit to stand trial," said the doctor.

Next on the stand was Dr. Tuchtie, from the Toronto Psychiatric Hospital, who said Smith was "mentally ill, suffering from a condition known as paranoid schizophrenia with delusions of persecution and grandeur."

During cross-examination, Langdon asked if Smith "was able to appreciate the nature of the act of bank robbery."

This touched off a back-and-forth debate between the witness and prosecutor about the proper definition of the word "appreciate." The courtroom tussle was one of several snippy exchanges during the doctor's testimony.

"It is not a fact that all [Smith] did was to behave like any other bank robber and that is to rob the banks and keep the money?" demanded the deputy Crown.

"I don't know. I'm not a bank robber and I wouldn't know, but certainly his own thinking and his driving force behind it, he was morally justified in doing this and getting the money. In his own mind he was doing something, and he was creating some chaos," snapped Dr. Tuchtie.

When Dr. Tuchtie left the stand, O'Driscoll announced he was done.

Langdon, however, had a medical expert of his own he was eager to put on the stand.

"I wish to call Dr. Easton in reply, my lord," said the deputy Crown.

Offering a drastically different diagnosis than his colleagues, Dr. Easton, an Ontario Hospital psychiatrist who had examined Smith, said Smith didn't suffer from schizophrenia and "was not insane last July." According to Dr. Easton, Smith had "an antisocial type of psychopathic personality."

A psychopath has "a deficient ethical and moral sense. The individual does not recognize the ordinary code of ethics that governs the behaviour of other members in the society in which he is living. He acts on his own completely. He tends to overreact to minor stimuli. He is devoid of feeling for others. He couldn't care less about the tragedy he brings on when he shoots another individual. He is shiftless, constantly changing his job and the area in which he is living," he explained.

This definition fit Smith, said the witness. Dr. Easton described Smith as the "dominant figure" and chief provider at Byng Avenue, handing out money and letting people stay for free.

During cross-examination, Dr. Easton conceded that heredity plays a role in schizophrenia and that he didn't know Smith's mother was schizophrenic (though he was aware she spent time in a psychiatric hospital). More damningly, Dr. Easton admitted that, prior to the trial, he hadn't been aware Smith had been diagnosed with schizophrenia in 1961.

To disprove the Crown's theory that Smith was psychopathic, O'Driscoll recited some of his client's statements to police. In these remarks, Smith took responsibility for his actions and expressed concern for other people. Were these the kind of sentiments someone with psychopathy — a condition marked by narcissism and refusal to admit guilt — typically displayed, asked the defence lawyer.

"It very well could be," offered Dr. Easton lamely.

The doctor also admitted that paranoid schizophrenics could show flashes of rationality.

O'Driscoll had no further questions. Judge Parker called a break, then O'Driscoll gave his closing statement.

"I submit to you, ladies and gentlemen, that on July the twenty-fourth, 1964, at about 5:10 p.m. Smith was insane within

Matthew Kerry Smith escorted by police on the day of his sentencing.

the meaning of Section 16 of the Criminal Code. If you accept the evidence that Smith is and was at the time of the shooting a paranoid schizophrenic … I submit to you, you must return with a verdict of not guilty by reason of insanity," said the defence lawyer.

He assured jurors that if they acquitted Smith, he would likely be institutionalized in a mental hospital. O'Driscoll repeated key points made by his defence experts and noted that Smith's mother was schizophrenic and residing at the Ontario Hospital.

"Ladies and gentlemen, I appeal to your minds, not to your hearts. I ask you not for mercy, but I ask you only for justice. I ask you to return a verdict: Not guilty by reason of insanity," he stated.

When it was Langdon's turn to offer closing remarks, he promised to be brief and kept his word. Smith was rational enough to plan the Bathurst Manor Plaza bank robbery and escape, then to remain at large for some time, said the deputy Crown. This proved Smith wasn't insane, he said. Langdon dismissed the Beatle

Bandit's revolutionary ideas and called him "a perfectly normal bank robber."

"Whether or not [Smith] may have had a disease of the mind, it is my further submission that his mind was not diseased to the extent that rendered him incapable of knowing that the act of bank robbery or shooting another person were wrong ... when Smith went into that bank on July the twenty-fourth of last year, he knew he was carrying a rifle, he knew he was robbing a bank, and when he shot and killed Blanc, he knew exactly what he was doing," stated the deputy Crown.

Langdon finished and Judge Parker adjourned the court. On the morning of May 19, the justice gave the jury some instructions, then sent them off to ponder a verdict. The jurors returned to the courtroom a little before noon with a verdict: "We find the accused guilty as charged," said the jury foreman.

Upon O'Driscoll's request, jury members were polled. Each juror said Smith was guilty.

"Ladies and gentlemen of the jury, you have found the accused guilty and the law requires that I now pronounce the sentence of death against him. Do you wish to make any recommendation as to whether or not he may be granted clemency?" asked Judge Parker.

The jury retired once again to discuss whether to recommend clemency, a request that might spare Smith from the noose. In under five minutes, the jury reached a conclusion. "No recommendation at all," said the jury foreman in court.

The judge told Smith to stand up.

"You have had a fair trial. You have been defended by very able counsel. Everything has been done on your behalf that could be done and the jury after due deliberation have reached the verdict that you have just heard that you are guilty of capital murder," stated Justice Parker.

He continued, using the same dry judicial language defendants in murder cases had come to dread.

"The sentence of the court, that you Matthew Kerry Smith, for the crime for which you have been found guilty, is that you be taken from the place where you are now to the place whence you came from, to be kept in close custody until the twenty-second day of September 1965, when you will be taken forth to the place of execution and hanged by the neck until you are dead and may God have mercy on your soul," said the judge.

Smith showed no emotion when the verdict was read. Nor did Eileen, who was in the courtroom watching.

"May I speak?" asked Smith.

"Yes," said the judge.

"I would just like to say what I have said before, about the overthrow of the government I believe in, and that I believe men will have to give their lives to change our government to fight decadence and to fight apathy. That is all," said Smith.

The prospect of death had done nothing to tamp down his fantasies about violent revolution.

Chapter Eight

Trouble Enough for a Lifetime

Following his conviction, Matthew Smith fell into the routines of prison life at the Don Jail in Toronto. He hand-wrote a series of letters to Eileen on prison stationery using a neat, cursive style. His letters were generally coherent and thoughtful, even if they did sometimes veer off on odd tangents.

"Dearest Eileen, What is the news with you these days? When you write next let me know if the baby, our son, is officially named and if his name is still Kerry. Also, let me know how he is and how you are getting along. Are you on welfare now and where are you living? You know I love you, but you can be honest with me whenever you decide to find another mate," wrote Smith on September 1, 1965.

The baby in question was Kerry Matthew Smith Junior, born July 7, 1965, and named in honour of his father. Smith was told about the birth by Don Jail governor Gerald Whitehead. The governor informed reporters that Smith was "quite happy" about the news. Smith's subsequent letters are filled with questions about his boy.

"I want to hear how our little genius is progressing and I am certain he will be a genius and at least smart enough to become a big chieftain and strong enough probably to beat any man up in town by the time he is a teenager," wrote Smith in early 1966.

At this point, Smith segued into a strange anecdote about his grandfather, who "could beat up almost any grown man by the age of ten and joined a circus at that age as an acrobat and muscle man."

It's unclear if this was a rare burst of wit on Smith's part or if he was indulging in his obsession with strength and masculinity.

In his letters, Smith fretted about Eileen's finances and demonstrated a paternal interest in Estelle ("don't forget to be an understanding and helpful parent to her," Smith wrote Eileen in a letter postmarked August 11, 1965). Another letter sent that same summer asked how Estelle was doing and whether she could "swim yet or nearly swim or just wade and splash."

When he wasn't writing about his family, Smith's communications focused on day-to-day concerns. He described his job sewing mailbags in the prison canvas workshop, his budding interest in crossword and jigsaw puzzles, and how he was reading the dictionary to improve his vocabulary and spelling.

One subject Smith didn't mention much was his impeding execution, now set for September 22. He did once write that his future was "in the hands of an appeal board, supreme court and cabinet. Their decision will make the future more clear." Otherwise, he had little to say about the matter.

While her boyfriend faced execution, Eileen herself no longer had to worry about going to jail. Along with Richard Skey, Joe Bashutzky, and her brother Kenneth, Eileen had been charged as an accessory to capital murder. After the quartet served as prosecution witnesses, these charges were dismissed in magistrate's court at the Crown's recommendation.

Warren John Laidlaw, for his part, had a considerably rougher time of it.

Shortly after Smith's arrest, his partner in the Sutton, Ontario, bank robbery gave himself up to police. In late June 1965, Laidlaw pleaded guilty to charges of bank robbery before York County Judge William Lyon in Toronto. At sentencing, the justice tore into Laidlaw.

"You were well aware that your co-conspirator was a bank robber who admitted to you that he had killed a person in a robbery," snapped Judge Lyon.

Laidlaw should still consider himself lucky, sniffed the justice. Laidlaw confessed it was his rifle that fired in the bank — accidentally, he insisted — wounding two people. Had either victim died, Laidlaw would have been charged with capital murder, said the judge. Since no one died in the robbery, Judge Lyon sentenced Laidlaw to five years in jail.

Laidlaw's arrest provided some closure to Mr. and Ms. Wales. The Waleses were the Toronto couple who unwittingly provided the getaway car for the Sutton robbery. The young woman who bought the Waleses' Meteor had falsely identified herself as Jackie Wilson. Now, the Waleses realized who she really was.

"'Jackie Wilson' was [Laidlaw's] wife. She is free but her baby won't have [their] daddy around for five long years. I liked her. Under different circumstances, we could have been friends," wrote Ms. Wales in a first-person account of the car-sale-gone-bad in the *Toronto Daily Star*.

While Smith penned letters and sewed mail bags, John O'Driscoll worked to save his client from the noose. O'Driscoll argued against Smith's conviction before a five-judge panel at the Ontario Court of Appeal on September 7.

Once again, O'Driscoll didn't deny that his client killed Jack Blanc. He appealed his client's conviction on two grounds. O'Driscoll insisted Smith was insane (and, therefore, shouldn't be hanged) and that Judge William Parker made errors in his instructions to jurors. The five justices mulled things over, then unanimously rejected both points.

"We are all of the opinion that there was no error in law in the learned trial judge's charge and that it was adequate under all the circumstances. As to the contention that the verdict of the jury in this issue is unreasonable or cannot be supported by the evidence, we are unanimously of the opinion that there was ample evidence to support the jury's conclusion and in particular to justify the jury's rejection of the appellant's allegation of insanity as defined in the Criminal Code. Notwithstanding the exceedingly able and comprehensive argument of counsel for the accused, we are of the opinion that the appeal must be dismissed," read a statement from Chief Justice Dana Porter, issued the same day O'Driscoll made his presentation.

This should have cleared the way for Smith to be hanged as planned, but a legal technicality forced a delay. Under the existing law, O'Driscoll had fifteen days to lodge a new appeal to the Supreme Court of Canada. The Ontario Court of Appeal had issued its ruling on September 7, however. Since Smith was scheduled to hang September 22, this meant his death would fall within the fifteen-day grace period.

To avoid undue complications, the federal justice department instructed the Ontario Attorney General's office to postpone the hanging. The extra time would allow O'Driscoll to prepare his appeal to the Supreme Court. Smith's execution date was moved to October 6, and O'Driscoll readied his notes for the Supreme Court of Canada hearing.

Smith had won a brief reprieve but on the face of it his situation still seemed grim. While no one had been executed in Canada in nearly three years, judges continued to hand out death sentences. In 1965, Canadian courts sentenced nineteen people, including Smith, to hang. The police and much of the public were strongly in favour of maintaining capital punishment.

This position was forcibly enunciated by Elmer Steeves, president of the Canadian Association of Chiefs of Police (CACP) at a conference in Niagara Falls, Ontario, that September.

"It is quite evident that the government — and this applies also to the previous administration at Ottawa — pays far more attention to the sob-sisters who are constantly interceding for dangerous criminals than they do for those who are responsible for maintaining law and order," snapped Steeves.

If his rhetoric was over the top, Chief Steeves was correct in noting that many elected officials were becoming wary about hanging criminals. The Progressive Conservatives commuted eleven death sentences in 1959, six in 1960, ten in 1961, and seven in 1962, according to government figures announced during House of Commons debate on June 14, 1965.

To capital punishment advocates, this was tantamount to surrender: "We pointed out to the government some time ago that appeasement with criminals was just as ineffective as it was with Hitler and his ilk and would reap the same results," said Chief Steeves at the CACP conference.

Attitudes were changing, however, and the Liberal Party — which took office in April 1963 after winning a federal election — stood firmly against the death penalty. Whereas the Conservatives had been somewhat choosy about commutations, the Liberals consistently intervened to prevent executions. Every death sentence passed after the Liberals took office was commuted.

Capital punishment remained on the books, however, and another change in government could easily mean another change in policy. Smith's supporters refused to get complacent.

"I can't afford to take for granted that they won't hang Kerry," said Matt Smith, in his *Globe and Mail* interview with Scott Young.

Smith Senior had offered to testify at his son's trial but was never called to the stand. When the trial concluded with a death sentence, Matt Smith threw himself into advocacy work. He also covered the legal fees for the trial and appeals.

"I remember my grandpa saying he would pay any amount of money to stop [his son] from being executed," recalls a now middle-aged Kerry Junior.

Matt Smith's poignant interview with Scott Young was published September 10 in the *Globe*. In an introduction to the interview, Young made it clear where he stood.

"After his son was arrested, he was approached many times by newspapers asking for details of his son's boyhood and youth. He had turned them all down in an attempt to preserve privacy for the rest of the family ... His motive in talking now is to add weight to his appeal that the Cabinet spare the life of his (he feels) insane son," wrote Young.

According to Young, Smith Senior also wanted to focus attention on the need to improve mental health services, so people like his son received the help they needed. In the article, Matt Smith fumed, "They wouldn't spend a few hundred to treat my son in 1961, but they'll spend tens of thousands to execute him after he finally killed somebody."

The newspaper story cast light on another Smith family tragedy. According to Young, Isabel Smith was too ill to understand what was happening with her child.

"When friends try to tell her of her son's date with the hangman, she had no understanding. She remarks that Kerry always has been a good boy, and isn't he doing well?" noted the *Globe*.

A *Globe* editorial published the day after the Matt Smith interview cast light on the issue of mental illness and the death penalty.

"Matthew Kerry Smith's father is convinced that his son is insane; so also, are some psychiatrists who examined him even before the crime was committed. If he is insane, he should not be hanged. So says the law," stated the editorial.

Nine days after these words were published, O'Driscoll filed his appeal with the Supreme Court of Canada.

"A spokesperson for Smith's family said ... the appeal is being launched 'in the belief that hanging is not the best possible treatment for mental illness,'" observed the *Globe*.

The move to grant Smith clemency began to gain momentum.

In early October, the Baptist Convention of Ontario and Quebec sent Prime Minister Lester Pearson a telegram asking him to set aside Smith's death sentence. An interfaith group called the Canadian Friends Service Committee gathered signatures on a petition to spare Smith. The petition was signed by top representatives of the Canadian Correctional Chaplaincy Association, the Society of Friends (Quakers), the Salvation Army Correctional Services, plus rabbis, ministers, and other religious leaders. Prominent trial lawyer Arthur Maloney, the president of the Canadian Society for the Abolition of the Death Penalty, spoke to the federal cabinet, requesting that Smith's sentence be commuted.

Against this backdrop of growing support for his client, O'Driscoll appeared before the Supreme Court of Canada on November 17. Opposing him was William Bowman, QC (Queen's Counsel), from the Department of the Attorney General. Interestingly, O'Driscoll and Bowman had faced off previously when Steven Truscott's conviction was reviewed by the Ontario Court of Appeal in 1960. That court ultimately rejected O'Driscoll's appeal.

While acknowledging his client was a killer, O'Driscoll said Smith "suffered from a disease of the mind that makes him incapable of knowing that the murder was morally wrong," wrote the *Globe and Mail*.

The defence lawyer asked the justices to grant a new trial or declare Smith not guilty by reason of insanity. He cited testimony from the defence experts and offered a pair of new affidavits from two other psychiatrists. The justices pondered the affidavits, then decided not to enter them into evidence.

Justice John Cartwright said it wasn't necessary to review new medical affidavits as the court "already had testimony of the four other doctors" who appeared at Smith's trial, reported the *Globe*.

The rejected affidavits were written by Dr. Arthur Blair, chief psychiatrist at the Ottawa Civic Hospital, and Dr. Gary Cormack, assistant superintendent and chief of staff at the Ontario Hospital. These doctors had visited Smith on separate occasions in September at the behest of the Department of Justice. No doubt, Justice officials hoped that the psychiatrists would buttress the Crown's contention that Smith was sane. The two doctors concluded the opposite.

"This 25-year-old man suffers from mental illness classified as schizophrenia of the paranoid type. With this prisoner, this illness has been characterized by abnormal thinking processes, a disordered stream of thought, delusions of grandeur and feelings of persecution ... This man is certifiably insane on the basis of his mental illness, let alone being a menace to society," wrote Dr. Blair in his affidavit.

"He has a mental sickness or disease of the mind known as schizophrenia ... this man would appear to be at the mercy of his psychosis ... This man is a danger not only to himself but to society and is certifiable under the Ontario Mental Hospitals Act," echoed Dr. Cormack.

It's not clear if these affidavits would have made a difference even if they had been entered into evidence. When it came time to deliberate, the justices discussed the case for less than ten minutes before coming to a decision.

"We are all of the opinion that the judgement of the Court of Appeal in this case is right. The appeal is therefore dismissed," stated Justice Cartwright, speaking for the court.

The man at the centre of the appeal was far from crushed by this decision. In a letter dated November 18, Smith expressed annoyance with O'Driscoll's legal stratagem, though not for reasons that might be expected.

"I am glad the Supreme Court of Canada upheld my conviction as I was always rather upset by people saying I'm nuts. Now they can only say that I'm a troublesome bank bandit and scoundrel. It is a mental relief to be designated a scoundrel rather than a screwball," Smith told Eileen.

Interestingly, Kerry Junior today states, about his father, "my mom never said he was crazy."

If pleased to be perceived as sane, Smith had no problem criticizing elements of Eileen's personality that annoyed him. When they lived together, Smith had frequently berated Eileen about her drinking habits. These sentiments became a reoccurring theme in his prison letters.

"Don't throw money away on liquor or partake of it needlessly. The kids need a good sober mother, and they need [security] love and understanding," wrote Smith.

A November 9 missive took a considerably snarkier tone: "When you are in the pub drinking beer, just think of ol' dry Matt here, smacking his lips for a cool beer. Of course, I can do without it even if I had it, but you can't," he stated.

Eileen suffered from addiction issues much of her adult life, but such harsh words were hardly justified, given her situation. When Smith was jailed, Eileen was largely left to her own devices, with no partner or financial support. She revealed the extent of her plight in an interview with the *Telegram* following Smith's arrest. To a *Tely* reporter, Eileen complained that police seized Smith's financial assets, leaving her broke. A sympathetic detective had to give her a couple of dollars just so she could afford food.

From his jail cell, Smith tried to help with finances, as best he could. In his August 17, 1965, letter, he told Eileen she was free to sell his car and tape recorder if she needed the cash. It's unclear if she followed through on this offer, though money was obviously tight. Smith also gave advice on social welfare programs Eileen might apply for to support herself.

As Smith adjusted to prison life, the federal government was springing into action. In response to questions by reporters in late November, Prime Minister Lester Pearson said cabinet would discuss Smith's case. Cabinet had to move fast.

"On December 8, a week from this Wednesday, one Matthew Kerry Smith will hang for murder unless the federal cabinet commutes his sentence," stated host Ed McGibbon, on a November 29, 1965, follow-up edition of the TV news program *Toronto File* devoted to the Beatle Bandit.

The episode featured a repeat of an interview salesman Hartley Lepofsky had given the year before on the same program.

Asked if he would vote to convict Smith of murder, knowing he would be executed as a result, Lepofsky had said, "I would find this a very difficult question to answer. There would have to be a great deal of thought given to it ... anyone who robs a bank with a gun would be classified as a murderer if someone was killed, because he has gone in there for armed robbery ... but actually, I don't think [Smith's] intent was to hurt anyone."

The same day the follow-up *Toronto File* episode aired the federal cabinet reached a decision. A communique was issued, which began as follows:

Whereas Matthew Kerry Smith, having been convicted of capital murder at Sittings of the Supreme Court of Ontario, held at the city of Toronto during the month of May 1965, and sentenced to be executed on the twenty-second day of September 1965, reprieved and execution of sentence postponed from time to time, by Order of the Court to the eighth day of December 1965.

Following more stodgy prose, came the words Smith's supporters had been hoping for: "His Excellency the Governor General in Council, pursuant to Section 656 of the Criminal Code, hereby commutes the sentence of death passed upon the prisoner to a term of life imprisonment in the Kingston Penitentiary."

The Beatle Bandit had been spared.

◆ ◆ ◆

The federal cabinet's decision outraged advocates of capital punishment, while delighting abolitionists. Critics were particularly incensed by the fact Smith was one of three convicted men to receive a commutation on the same day.

"The Beatle Bandit, a bomb killer and a sex murderer were the latest convicted murderers to escape the hangman's noose," stated *The Winnipeg Tribune*.

The bomb killer was Joseph Letourneau, who had murdered a man over a land transaction by fitting a homemade explosive device to his Jeep. The sex murderer was Leopold Dion, convicted of killing a thirteen-year-old boy during a sexual assault, and suspected of committing other violent crimes. Both men were from Quebec. Dion had been scheduled to hang December 5 while Letourneau's execution was slated for December 10.

According to the *Tribune*, the decision marked "19 straight commutations in a row under the Pearson government."

The *Star* and the *Globe and Mail* editorialized in favour of the triple commutation.

"The Cabinet has acted rightly in commuting to life imprisonment the death sentences passed on Toronto Beatle bandit Matthew Kerry Smith and two other convicted murderers. Prime Minister Lester Pearson has promised that a free vote on the retention of capital punishment will be held shortly after Parliament convenes; and it would be intolerable that men be hanged while the country examines its conscience about the rightness of such an action," noted the *Globe*.

The commutation trend didn't mean killers would walk free, the *Globe* reassured readers. Under changes to parole regulations implemented in late 1964, commuted murderers could only be paroled with the permission of the federal cabinet.

"The federal government has acted wisely in commuting the death sentences of three criminals," echoed the *Star*.

Law enforcement officials and some elected politicians expressed extreme misgivings. James Mackey, who was president of the Canadian Association of Chiefs of Police, as well as Metropolitan Toronto police chief, fired off an angry letter to the minister of justice. He repeated some of his remarks to members of the media.

"Smith is a vicious killer. I can't see how treatment can ever change him," said Chief Mackey, as reported by the *Montreal Gazette*.

The *Star* editorial cited the same quote but added its own riposte: "Whether or not there is a chance of rehabilitating Smith, the real issue is not the fate of this single man, but rather the usefulness of capital punishment as an instrument of justice in a civilized society."

For all that, the *Gazette* noted that even some members of the Liberal government opposed the decision. Ralph Cowan (Liberal MP — York Humber, Ontario), for one, accused cabinet of "usurping the power of the courts in commuting death sentences," wrote the paper.

"A judge in handing down his decision has to give reasons. But Cabinet never gives reasons for upsetting the law of the land," said Cowan, a capital-punishment supporter.

Columnist Ron Collister, who was published in newspapers nationwide, criticized the Liberals for not subjecting capital punishment to a vote in the House of Commons.

"What right does the government have to abolish the death penalty, in effect before Parliament has spoken? ... Is commutation being used as a safe way out of difficult situations where, on technical grounds, evidence of insanity cannot be admitted in appeal courts, evidence that conceivably could save the condemned killer?" asked Collister.

Collister cited the Smith case, noting that the Supreme Court refused to review affidavits that declared he was "certifiably insane under the Ontario Medical Hospitals Act."

This column was published in the *Brandon Sun* in Manitoba and *The Daily Colonist* in Victoria, B.C., among other newspapers, evidence that the commutations caused a national uproar.

The decisions to spare Smith, Letourneau, and Dion marked a turning point. It was increasingly obvious that the Liberals weren't making any exceptions to their no-hanging policy. In 1967, legislation was passed suspending most executions for five years. While murdering a police officer or jail guard was still punishable by hanging, the Liberal government continued to commute all other new death sentences.

The moratorium on executions was renewed after the initial five-year suspension came to an end. The death penalty was officially removed from the Criminal Code following a narrow vote in the House of Commons in July 1976. Members of the military could still, theoretically, be executed for treason or mutiny, but this punishment wasn't applied. The National Defence Act was amended in December 1998 to abolish death sentences for the military as well.

Having escaped the noose, Smith was transferred to Kingston Penitentiary in early December. Located in Kingston, Ontario and open since 1835, this maximum-security prison was one Canada's most notorious penal institutions. Dubbed an "archaic dungeon" at a 1966 inquest, the Kingston Pen housed some of the toughest convicts in the country. It was the scene of a murderous prison riot in 1971.

Smith was again given a job sewing mailbags. He dropped by the prison library on occasion and accepted visits from a chaplain. Smith attended Salvation Army services once a week and continued to be questioned by doctors and psychiatrists.

"Most of the time, we are in our cells, but we can do hobby-craft and reading or listen to the radio on our earphones. I am four stories up on a range of cells above the floor and the opening and closing of these cells all occurs to the sound of a bell from a circular shaped dome in the center of the prison. It is difficult but I am gradually getting used to the steady routine here," wrote Smith, in a letter to Eileen postmarked January 22, 1966.

Eileen occasionally wrote back. Smith also received letters from his parents. Smith Senior and Lianne kept in contact with Eileen as well, to bolster her spirits.

During his time in the Kingston Penitentiary, Smith became gripped by the notion that his mental illness stemmed from physical causes. Perhaps the head injury he suffered in the navy caused lesions or abnormalities that changed his personality? Taking this line of reasoning a step further, Smith wondered if brain surgery might return to him to normality. Once fixed, perhaps he could be transferred to Manitoba to serve the rest of his sentence. Eileen had gone back to Elphinstone, where she was raising Estelle and Kerry Junior. Smith figured he could see his family if he, too, went West. It was a considerable change in attitude, given Smith had previously criticized O'Driscoll for portraying him as insane.

Smith expressed some of these thoughts in his letters. In an undated letter with a March 30, 1966, postmark, Smith told Eileen that he had "mastosis, which is simply a mastoid (which most healthy people have) located behind the ear in my head and it is defective."

Had this defective mastoid been detected and operated on earlier, Smith said his brain power would have soared: "Instead of a normal IQ which I have now, I could have instead an intelligence far higher than Einstein," he wrote.

In a follow-up letter, Smith almost causally noted that doctors had decided they didn't need to operate after all.

While brain-enhancing surgery was just another delusion, Smith apparently was quite serious about something else. If newspaper accounts are accurate, the Beatle Bandit concluded that violence was not, after all, justified as a means of achieving social change.

"He was filled with a sense of shame at what he had done, he wrote, and destroyed newspaper accounts of his crimes and trial. The only one he kept was an article on his life written by *Globe and Mail* columnist Scott Young last September," wrote the *Globe and Mail*.

To most of the outside world, however, Smith was still a homicidal maniac and a cautionary tale. This position was driven home by an alarming article in the national publication *Maclean's* magazine. Unsubtly titled "The Menace of Insane Killers at Large," the article offered a jeremiad against the judicial and medical system: "There are too many potentially dangerous people at large in the community. They are walking around, as one psychiatrist puts it, 'like loaded bombs,' and it is obvious that the legal and institutional machinery we have devised to prevent explosions is inadequate for the job."

Smith and Leopold Dion were held out as examples of dangerous people at large. The piece acknowledged that Smith had received some treatment for schizophrenia at the Toronto Forensic Clinic in 1961. Nonetheless, the writer argued, Smith and others of his ilk should have been kept under closer watch.

"In every case, the offenders had given abundant warning of mental disturbance. In every case they had received some kind of institutional attention, but when the institution was finished with them, there was no follow-up," huffed *Maclean's*.

Smith made the pages of the same magazine a year later, in a totally different story that lamented the lack of vocational opportunities for Canadian prisoners. Smith wanted to take courses to earn certification as a stationary engineer — that is, a person responsible for maintaining industrial and power-generating machinery, explained *Maclean's*. His dreams of academic achievement were nixed by prison officials. They apparently were concerned that

Smith would have nothing else to look forward to, should he obtain a stationary engineering certificate so early in his sentence.

Engineering certificate or not, life went on behind bars.

Smith penned a light-hearted Valentine's Day note in mid-February 1966 addressed to Eileen, Estelle, and Kerry Junior: "I send my three favorite sweethearts all my love; today, Valentine's Day. Also, Eileen, can you think of any little gift I could make for the kiddies for their birthdays from hobbycraft? I just started studying music here and soon may be playing a guitar and letting my hair grow long," wrote Smith.

Despite such playful notes, Smith continued to obsess about physical ailments and was examined by multiple doctors. Smith visited the prison medical centre, complaining about headaches and a clicking sound in his ear. Dr. William Amodeo, who worked as the prison physician, could find nothing wrong with him. Smith was given an electroencephalogram test, just to be sure. It indicated that Smith might be vulnerable to seizures, except that he never had seizures, so this wasn't an issue.

If Smith was physically okay, Dr. Amodeo wasn't so sure about his mental health. The doctor noticed that Smith tended to ramble during conversations. In April, Dr. Robert McCaldon, the second psychiatrist working at the Kingston Penitentiary, placed Smith on medication (according to the *Globe*, the drug in question was Librium, an anxiety-reducing sedative).

Dr. Amodeo wrote a report about Smith that made its way to Dr. George Scott, the Kingston Penitentiary's chief psychiatrist. Dr. Scott was already aware of Smith's condition, having previously examined him.

Dr. Scott believed Smith was "close to schizophrenic" but didn't recommend placing him in the prison psychiatric wing, wrote the *Globe*. Prisoners in that wing weren't given regular work duties, and doing work helped keep Smith focused, reasoned the doctor.

Not focused enough, it turned out.

♦ ♦ ♦

In the early morning of June 13, 1966, Correctional Officer John Reid performed a routine patrol inside the Kingston Penitentiary. During his rounds, Reid checked each cell. The CO estimated he passed by Cell 14, Block G, fourth range — the cell housing Smith — around 3:20 or 3:35 a.m. When the correctional officer peered inside, all seemed fine.

One of Reid's subordinates, a correctional officer named Douglas Glenn, carried out the next patrol. He looked into Smith's cell at 5:30 a.m. and quickly realized something was amiss. For a start, Glenn couldn't see the prisoner though he did see lots of blood. The alarmed correctional officer swept his flashlight beam around the cell and saw that Smith was lying on the floor. Glenn immediately summoned Alan Riley, the hospital attendant at the Kingston Pen.

Reid let Riley inside Cell 14, where Smith lay on his back, his head near the toilet. Smith's left arm was on his chest and his left wrist was slashed and bleeding. Smith had no pulse and Riley didn't think he was breathing.

The walls, floor, and toilet in the cell were coated in blood. Riley raced to the prison hospital, grabbed a syringe of adrenalin, and administered it to the prostrate prisoner. Despite the blast of adrenalin, there was still no pulse or other response from Smith.

Kingston police were notified, and Detective James Sheridan arrived around seven to examine Smith's body. The detective inspected the cell and discovered the sheets on Smith's cot were soaked in blood. Det. Sheridan also found a piece of a razor blade and four intact razor blades in their wrappers on a table.

Dr. Amodeo, who also examined Smith in his cell, discovered that he had made cuts on the underside of his left wrist and on his forearm. Noting that rigor mortis had not set in, Dr. Amodeo figured Smith had been dead for maybe three or four hours by the time he was discovered.

An autopsy was performed, and the cause of death was given as heart failure, due to extreme loss of blood. Convicts housed near Smith were questioned and said they heard nothing. Nobody reported hearing signs of distress, pain, or anger as Smith lay dying.

For all the appeals, petitions, and high-level political discussions to keep him alive, the Beatle Bandit was now dead, by his own hand.

◆ ◆ ◆

If Smith had been placed in the psychiatric wing at Kingston Penitentiary, he wouldn't have had easy access to safety razors. Since Smith wasn't in this wing, however, he had both a razor and razor blades in his cell.

In a scathing article for the *Globe*, Scott Young noted that Doctors Blair and Cormack had deemed Smith to be a suicide risk. Young questioned why Smith was housed among the general population, when he clearly should have been in the prison psychiatric wing.

"No matter how Smith appeared by day, did they have to leave him in his cell night after night, including the sad hours of the early morning which many prisoners say are the worst of all, all the time possessing a razor blade?" wrote Young.

Since Smith's violent death occurred in a public institution, an inquest was mandatory. The inquest took place July 13 in the Frontenac County courthouse in Kingston, presided over by coroner Dr. Stuart Patterson. Various prison officials testified. The five-man jury discussed matters, then concluded that Smith had indeed killed himself. While that was hardly in doubt, the jury also said prison staff weren't negligent and that Smith had received adequate medical care.

Another investigation followed the coroner's inquest. Smith's brain was removed and carefully analyzed in a lab. Doctors wanted to see if Smith really did suffer from physical injuries that impaired his judgment and made him prone to violent behaviour. No such injuries or defects were found.

◆ ◆ ◆

As to why Smith ended his own life, no one knows. His letters to Eileen and to his lawyer make no mention of suicide.

"Quite often, I received letters from Smith. He gave no indication of depression. In fact, he seemed quite happy," stated O'Driscoll, in the *Telegram*.

In one letter to Eileen postmarked October 6, 1965, Smith wrote, "I am lonely, sick and dispairing [sic]. But I love you. Bye Love. Matt."

This was an unusual departure for him, as most of his letters were upbeat or made no mention of his mood. Even Smith himself seemed aware of this; in the same anomalous missive, he states, "PS. When I write next, I will try to write a more lengthy letter, more sensibly and cheerful so please excuse this little letter."

If O'Driscoll was baffled by his client's death, others weren't quite as surprised. The *Telegram* ran a story about the inquest with the headline "Beatle Bandit's Suicide Almost Inevitable, Jury Told." The piece quoted Crown Attorney John E. Sampson, whose address to inquest jurors made it clear he accepted the majority medical opinion about Smith's condition.

Smith was a "borderline schizophrenic who, I believe, could not face the utter hopelessness of his situation at Kingston Penitentiary," said Sampson.

The *Globe and Mail* offered more of the Crown attorney's remarks in the same vein.

Referencing the Kingston Pen, Sampson said, "It's old, very nearly an archaic dungeon. It contains over 900 of the worst criminals in Canada. To Smith, it must have seemed like the end of the road and he took it," wrote the *Globe*.

A wistful column in the *Globe* by Scott Young, styled like a letter from Kingston Penitentiary, expanded on this theme.

"So, Matthew Kerry Smith came here in December. He had Christmas with us. No joy, I assure you. He looked around and didn't seem to be impressed with what he saw ... He looked around at the other lifers, hundreds of them, many in their twenties like him. He saw nothing encouraging in their faces. He spoke to them and found nothing encouraging in their minds," wrote Young.

"Parole was his only hope. Being realistic, he acknowledged 15 years as the minimum. That's 5,480 mornings without hope. A period of time equal to about three-fifths of his life ... The past was an open mess. The present, intolerable. The future held no promise. He stayed six months, looked it over pretty carefully and made his decision. Two quick deep slashes to let the blood run. No sound. No cry for help. No changing his mind. He died quietly without bothering anyone," continued Young.

Another possible explanation for Smith's death comes from the boy he fathered before entering prison: "I always have thoughts about the reason he committed suicide. I think that it's because he killed Jack Blanc. It probably replayed in his head over and over and probably was too much for him. That's just my thought on it. I'm sure he was wracked with remorse about it. It probably ate him up. I presume he would have a lot of time in prison to think about it," states Kerry Junior.

Chapter Nine

Postscript

As friends and family looked on, a granite headstone honouring Jack Blanc was unveiled at Mount Sinai Cemetery on October 3, 1965. Rabbi David Monson presided over the event, alongside Rabbi Aaron Zimmerman and Harvey Lister, president of the General Wingate Legion Branch.

The dark, imposing tombstone was rectangular in shape, with an engraved Star of David and Blanc's name at the top in capital letters. Beneath his name were words of praise in English and Hebrew. The English portion read, in part, "In loving memory of my devoted husband and our dear father Jack Blanc, a heroic soldier with the Canadian and Israeli armies who sacrificed his life in aiding the police to protect the public ... How the courageous have fallen."

In the days following Blanc's death, police officers checked in on his wife and son. They came for information and to provide comfort and protection. With Jack Blanc's killer still at large, authorities didn't know if he would return to attack the family.

After her husband was killed, Sally Blanc received about $150 a month from the Canadian Bankers Association in compensation. It wasn't a huge amount, given her husband had been earning around

$200 a week (worth roughly eight-and-a-half times as much today, factoring inflation) as a fur-cutter, according to his son. But the financial pain was nothing compared to the family's emotional devastation.

"My mother went downhill right away. She never really recovered," recalls Stanley.

Stanley struggled at school and moved with his mother to a different neighbourhood. Sally Blanc died "ten years after my father, same month — she died July 9, 1974," recalls Stanley.

Stanley took courses at Toronto-area colleges, then worked various jobs at a bookstore and with a customs broker. A senior citizen now, he has crystal-clear memories of his father.

"He wasn't religious — we didn't even have a Hanukkah menorah in the house or Hebrew scriptures — but he knew what was right … There was right and there was wrong. That doesn't mean he was always perfect, but he believed in right from wrong. You don't steal, you don't rob, you don't kill people," says Stanley.

Killing people in warfare is sometimes unavoidable, but that is different than murdering people while committing a crime, he says, adding, "You don't rob banks and kill people."

Asked about Matthew Kerry Smith, Stanley says, "I feel he was a sick man. He was mentally ill … but I also think there was a bit of evil in there. What makes me upset, for his sake, they still had a hospital for the criminally insane in Penetanguishene. That's where he should have gone. He shouldn't have gone to Kingston, that was a big mistake."

Stanley suggests his father's actions might have been a post-traumatic response to the sound of gunfire.

Smith let off a warning shot in the bank and "I think that it gave my father shell shock. Otherwise, he wouldn't have done it," states Stanley.

Stanley offers a special memory about his father. On the evening of April 20, 1961, some 2,500 people gathered in Massey Hall in Toronto to commemorate the thirteenth anniversary of the state of Israel. Described as "Israel's Bar Mitzvah," the event featured speeches, awards, and a presentation.

At one point, a group of former Jewish soldiers who had served in the Canadian Army or Israeli forces came on stage. They were led by Jack Blanc, who had not lost his drill-instructor abilities or commanding tone.

"There was silence, and I hear this voice, 'Ten, hut!' and they come marching out. That was wonderful," recalls Stanley, who was watching proudly with his mother in the audience.

"He was a good person," adds Stanley.

Eileen also tried to carry on as best she could, following her loss.

"From what my mom told me, after my dad went to prison, she was left by herself, with no family, so she moved back to Manitoba," reports Kerry Junior.

In her hometown of Elphinstone, Eileen looked after her children. There were three of them now — Estelle, Kerry Junior, and Wagner, who was born shortly after Smith's death following a relationship with a new partner. With little money coming in, Eileen's situation was grim.

Things changed for the better thanks to a visit by the Beatle Bandit's mother. Like her son, Isabel Smith enjoyed periods of lucidity when her schizophrenia receded, and at this point her mind was relatively clear. Isabel was living with her sister Ruth Crichton in Saskatchewan and decided to pay Eileen a visit. Eventually coming to be known as Grandma Belle, or simply grandma, on that first visit she was appalled by the living conditions in Eileen's residence.

Isabel reported what she saw to her sister. According to Isabel, Eileen was "stuffing newspapers in holes in the walls to keep the snow out and the kids were sleeping in boxes and they were in dire poverty," recalls Cindy Griffiths, who became Eileen's daughter-in-law in the late 1980s.

Given that Isabel had been diagnosed with schizophrenia, Ruth was skeptical at first. Once Eileen's plight was confirmed, though, the Crichton and Smith families sprang into action. Smith Senior and Ruth arranged for the purchase of a house to accommodate Eileen and her kids. The house was in Saskatoon, Saskatchewan, and the family moved in during the summer of 1969.

"I really loved that house ... it was two storeys. It's 106 years old now. I had a very bright pink room. It was a hot room in winter and the coolest room in summer," states Estelle.

There was further assistance, contact, and love from the Smith and Crichton families. Eileen, however, remained mired in alcohol and unemployment. On social assistance most of her life, she achieved periods of sobriety but struggled with alcoholism. Kerry and Estelle do not gloss over their family history, nor do they condemn their mother.

"It was really tough growing up ... We knew our mom tried the best she could," says Estelle.

"I guess we weren't rich. I don't know — we were fine the way we were. We didn't know any different," echoes Kerry.

Growing up, the children in the family were close. They didn't view each other as half-siblings with different dads, but as brothers and sister, continues Kerry Junior.

Eileen didn't talk much about Matthew Kerry Smith's criminal activities. She kept in close touch with his father and sister, however. Both Matt Smith and Lianne corresponded with Eileen following the Beatle Bandit's death. Eileen wrote back on occasion.

One of the few letters Eileen left behind is dated April 6, 1976, and addressed to Smith Senior and his second wife, Anne Bartley Smith. Anne was a well-known journalist and magazine editor who previously had gone by the last name Fromer.

"Dear Matt and Anne, Thank you very much for asking to send Kerry and Wagner to school for a year. I have thought about it and had decided just to let them visit," writes Eileen.

The letter doesn't say, but presumably Eileen is referring to an offer from Matt Smith to fund a private-school education. Eileen was hesitant, stating, "we would miss them very much" if the boys left home to attend school.

At this point in the letter, Eileen holds out the possibility of a family visit with Kerry and Wagner. Eileen implies that her boys can be a handful and that she "plays bingo at night" to give herself some private time.

"Maybe a visit from both of them would be better too when they're a bit older. We can arrange for them to go to camp here if they don't visit you. Thank you again for your kindness. We all think of you often. Love Eileen and family," concludes the letter.

Visits did occur between Eileen's children and the Smith family. Kerry recalls a time Matt Smith took him and brother Wagner to dinner at Bonanza, a popular steakhouse named after the TV show. Kerry was around seven or eight at the time.

"Bonanza had these big wooden beams that went across [the ceiling]. [Matt Smith] jumps up on one of these beams and starts doing chin-ups. My brother and I kind of looked at each other and went —" at this point, Kerry breaks into a laugh.

Kerry got along well with Smith Senior, noting that "he actually tested me when I was a kid."

Kerry recalls a time when Matt Smith deliberately left coins in plain view at his home to see if he would steal them. Kerry Junior didn't abscond with the money "because he was my grandfather" — earning the man's respect.

Kerry says he also enjoyed a warm relationship with the Beatle Bandit's sister and her husband.

As a boy, he became known as Kerry Griffiths, not Kerry Smith. While unsure about the legal specifics, Kerry Junior says, "my grandpa Matt got my name changed when I was ten years old, nine years old."

For his part, Matt Smith became wealthy as a property developer. He and Anne lived in Aurora, Ontario.

Estelle recalls visiting the couple when she was around twelve. She says, "they were both very gracious" and she enjoyed seeing them. Estelle has no memories at all of Matthew Kerry Smith and few recollections of living at 213 Byng Avenue.

Eileen married again in July 1977, to a Richard MacDonald. The two had a son together, called Ryan.

When Anne Bartley Smith died December 1, 1987, "she left a magnificent country estate to a provincial heritage group," noted the *Star*. The large property became a source of contention between groups that wanted to build houses on it and groups that wanted it preserved in a bucolic state.

Prior to his own death, Smith Senior established a trust fund for Eileen's children. Estelle used her share to attend school, graduating with a four-year degree in Native Studies and a history minor from the University of Saskatchewan in 1990.

Scott Young — the *Globe* reporter who eloquently related Matt Smith's anguish — enjoyed a lengthy writing career but is primarily remembered today for being the father of rock star Neil Young.

Isabel Smith died in 1992. She was buried in the Rosedale Cemetery in her hometown of Moose Jaw. A Crichton family tombstone, which also marks her father, mother, and siblings, refers to her as "Isabelle Smith."

Estelle maintained a loving, if sometimes strained, relationship with her mother. She acknowledges that her academic achievements set her apart from Eileen, who never finished grade school. By the same token, Estelle never drank alcohol until she was forty years old, never married, and is intensely focused on work. Estelle lives in Saskatoon, near the home purchased for her family in 1969, and holds down multiple jobs. She works as caretaker of an apartment block, has a cleaning job with city transit, and does private cleaning services on weekends.

Estelle thinks it's fine for hunters, police officers, and soldiers to have guns, but otherwise has no interest in firearms and doesn't like violence.

Kerry Junior married his high-school sweetheart Cindy in 1988. At the time, she had known her partner only as Kerry Griffiths, so it was decided to stick with that family name instead of Smith.

In 1991, Kerry used his portion of the Matt Smith trust fund to buy a home in a tiny village in Saskatchewan. For a time, Kerry and Cindy — who both had food industry experience — ran an area restaurant together. Kerry was the cook while Cindy worked as a waitress. The young couple had two little children by this point, so Eileen moved into their home to babysit.

"Eileen stayed here and looked after the kids while we worked. The neighbours were kind of scared of her when they first met her, like I was. But the minute they got to know her, she was the most kind, loving person," says Cindy.

Things didn't go quite as planned with the restaurant, so Kerry and Cindy left the business and took other jobs. Kerry worked for a plant-based bio-tech company while Cindy took a position as a teller at a credit union. The family embraced Kerry's Indigenous heritage and frequently visited friends and relatives at First Nations communities. They spent time at Keeseekoowenin Ojibway First Nation near Elphinstone ("my mother's reserve," notes Kerry) and the Rolling River First Nation near Erickson, Manitoba.

Richard MacDonald died May 1, 2005. Five years later, Eileen was hospitalized with cancer. Her daughter was in the same hospital, also being treated for cancer. Eileen died July 28, 2010, and was buried in Glenside, Saskatchewan. A gravestone features Richard's name followed by that of Eileen (her name is given as Eileen Charity MacDonald). An engraved pair of stylized turtles flank the dates marking her birth and death, symbols of her Indigenous heritage.

A decade later, the Beatle Bandit's sister, Lianne, died. Her obituary, posted on the Find A Grave website, notes that she married a medical doctor, had three children, attended Victoria University (a college of the University of Toronto), and worked as a public school teacher. The obituary cites Lianne's Christian faith. She died at age eighty-three in a town in the southern United States, on August 27, 2019.

Cindy Griffiths retired from the credit union at the end of 2020. Her final position involved being "the accountant for all the accountants," as she puts it.

Kerry's firm was bought out by a cannabis company, where he remains employed.

Growing up, Kerry was fearful he might become schizophrenic like his father. He recalls being tested by a psychiatrist when he was nine or so. As he grew older and showed no sign of developing schizophrenia, he worried that his children might inherit the condition. Fortunately, his kids never developed it, either.

Kerry Junior remains curious about his lineage.

"I wish I had got to know my dad. My grandpa used to talk about him every once in a while," states Kerry.

Eileen would occasionally tell stories about his father, without offering details about his crimes, he continues.

As to what kind of stories, Kerry says simply, "Well, that she was in love with my dad and my dad was in love with her."

Estelle has similar memories about her mother. Eileen liked to say "that we don't always know who we fall in love with. My mother was very accepting of everyone. I know in some of the [prison] letters, there's a private joke that only Matt Kerry Smith and my mom knew. She never discussed it, but she would get a smile. She seemed to be happy," recalls Estelle.

Estelle doesn't have children. Kerry and Cindy have a daughter, a son, and two granddaughters whom they dote on. Kerry says his children were not aware their grandfather was a bank robber until he was contacted by Paul Truster, who performed the preliminary research for this book. At that point, Kerry had to inform his kids about their notorious grandfather.

Kerry and Cindy's daughter didn't wish to be mentioned in this book, for reasons of privacy. Their boy — the Beatle Bandit's grandson — is named Matthew. This is a way of preserving the family name.

"The family name of Matthew has carried on to four generations. There's Matthew Bartley, Matthew Kerry, then my brother Kerry Matthew, and he has a son named Matthew," states Estelle.

Matthew served in the Canadian navy. Unlike his grandfather, he completed his enlistment term. Matthew currently works as a millwright, "a jack-of-all-trades," according to his mother, and is doing fine.

Afterword

The early evening of July 24, 1964, stands out indelibly in my childhood memory — specifically, the moment when my father, arriving home from work, walked up our driveway and, finding me playing on the lawn, announced, "A man's been killed up at the plaza."

The man was Jack Blanc, whom I'd met about a month earlier, at the YMHA swimming pool off Bathurst Street in North York. I dimly remember holding back shyly when a man volunteered to teach my brother and me how to dive properly. That, my father reminded me, was Jack Blanc.

Our family had been among the thousands who moved to Bathurst Manor soon after it was converted from farmland to a Fifties suburb on the Levittown model. The bulk of the newcomers were Jewish. They were of two kinds. Some were expats from the downtown Toronto ghetto that had grown out of the earlier slum known as the Ward. Others were survivors of Hitler's genocide. Many of their non-Jewish neighbours likewise had grim memories of the Depression and the war. All thought of the Manor as an island of relative comfort and safety, which it was. But if they had left behind violence and the fear of violence, violence obligingly came to them that July evening. Matthew Kerry Smith, himself a North York boy, robbed a bank at Wilmington Avenue and Overbrook Place, holding a rush-hour crowd of patrons in terror, and sparking the Wild-West-style duel that ended in Blanc's death.

The immediate impact on the Manor wasn't entirely dissimilar to that of President Kennedy's assassination the previous November. Many neighbourhood people of a certain age still say, "I remember exactly where I was when I heard that Jack Blanc was killed," just as they do of JFK. The plaza's custodian told me that people who had long since left the Manor, on visiting years later, would lift their young children up to let them feel around the bullet hole that was still visible in the plaza's metal box sign. The sign and the plaza were leveled a few years ago, but the curious can still see the death scene on the lawn of 118 Overbrook Place. Blanc fell between the two trees that still serve as markers. They were little more than saplings then — no serious obstacle to the shooter standing fifteen meters away, on the west side of Elder Street.

But while people remembered the day, its details became fuzzier with time, re-emerging as folklore and myth. Smith, it was averred, was an American — no respectable Canadian robber would have worn so macabre a costume, much less leapt up on a bank counter, rifle in hand. (How soon they had forgotten Edwin Alonzo Boyd, who had done the same a few miles away and a dozen years earlier! But Smith, who devoured newspaper crime stories as a boy, had not forgotten.)

Some said Smith had been apprehended in Texas, hanging himself in his cell before he could be extradited. He was said to have used a Tommy-gun to kill Blanc, to have laughed as he gunned him down, and to have escaped with a partner. These were all fictions, like those that affixed themselves to Wyatt Earp, Billy the Kid, and Bonnie and Clyde; though readers of this book will recognize shards of the truth embedded in the fictions.

This most bizarre of Canadian crime stories — including the continent-wide manhunt, the trial, the struggle to commute the death sentence, and Smith's suicide in Kingston Penitentiary — was a national story for nearly two years. It always fascinated me, not least because I walked by the bank, and that haunting bullet hole, almost daily on my way to and from school. My parents, like the Blancs, had accounts there, and I must often have seen Carman Lamb, Henry Martens, and the brave "first teller," Joan Hoffman.

In 2002 I became seriously interested in untangling what was true and what wasn't in all the garbled accounts. Initially, I didn't even recall whether Smith had died or been paroled. I said to my wife, Heather, "Maybe we could have him over to dinner!" "Not in *my* house," she replied. But she soon became nearly as absorbed as I was in the search, which took us through Library and Archives Canada, the Archives of Ontario, the Toronto Police Museum, and, in search of anyone with memories to share, to Sutton West; Halifax; Saskatoon; Delta, B.C.; and Camden, Arkansas.

It had become obvious to us that this neglected gem among Canadian crime stories deserved to be told in full. But the years passed, the planned book went unwritten. My seven bankers' boxes of documents and photographs gathered dust, a guilt-inducing monument of the kind only too familiar to hard-core procrastinators. The problem was solved only in 2019 when, after reading Nate Hendley's fine true-crime book *The Boy on the Bicycle*, I tracked him down and asked him to give me twenty minutes over coffee. Authors are constantly being approached by well-meaning people who "have a great idea for your next book," so I was relieved when Nate, with just a touch of wariness, agreed to meet. Happily, he was soon persuaded, both by the inherent interest of the story and by the unusual profusion of surviving documentation — catnip for authors. Supplementing this with his own diligent research and interviews, he turned my formless dream into the expert account you are holding.

But why should any of this matter now, over half a century after the close of the Beatle Bandit's brief and violent life?

It's true that, as Nate shows, the story opens a window into a time that is both like and unlike our own. The practice of keeping guns in banks ended soon after Blanc's death, which was almost certainly responsible for the change. That seems very distant now, and the once-fierce debate on the death penalty scarcely less so. But issues of mental illness and criminal responsibility remain relevant, and prison reform is very much on the public agenda.

For me, though, the story's primary interest today is not as a subject of historical or sociological inquiry, but as a tragedy, one that that has lost none of its disconcerting power. Ungainly and episodic as it is, laced with startling and macabre incidents, it bears overall the unmistakable, ironic symmetry of Greek tragedy. And like all great tragedies, it is built on the interplay of character and chance, or Fate.

For all their differences, Blanc, the man who served his country in war and died defending his community in peacetime, and Smith, the antisocial robber claiming the justification of hazy revolutionary ideals, turn out to have been remarkably alike in ways that drive the tragedy.

Both were loners who yet managed to be husbands and fathers.

Both served in the military and, beyond any doubt, defined themselves above all as warriors.

Both wrestled with the problem of giving adequate expression to their warrior impulses in the comparatively peaceable world of early-1960s North America. And the overwhelming need to do so, joined to massive ill luck, brought these two perfect strangers into a momentary acquaintance that destroyed them both.

Smith's and Blanc's need to assert themselves as warriors was not theirs alone. It seems to speak to something with very deep roots, not only in a particular culture but in the human mind (I would say, in the masculine mind, especially). Society, until recently at least, has rarely been entirely at ease with the soldier; still less with the gunfighter, bandit, or gangster. But from Homer to Hollywood, the romantic aura that envelops them is too common and too obvious to miss. We disapprove of, or withhold full approval from, the violent man. But most of us have a corner of our brains in which we admire the boldness and courage of those who willingly put their lives on the line, whatever their motives.

Around 1325, an anonymous Icelandic author wrote a saga about an outlaw named Grettir, who in some ways resembles Matthew Kerry Smith in particular. Two of the saga's modern editors describe a self-willed boy who "defies, violently, cruelly and wittily, the authority of his father." While still in his teens he kills a man and is sentenced to outlawry, "perhaps his natural state." Brave but self-destructive, with an "obsessional feeling that he must ... keep proving his superiority," Grettir ends his life in isolation on a rocky island, having "gone too far on a path that takes him inexorably apart from other men." He "cannot live in society, yet he cannot bear living away from it." For all his obvious character defects he remains an anti-hero, which is, after all, a kind of hero.*

If Carman Lamb had chambered a fifth bullet in the bank revolver Blanc used, and had that bullet killed Smith, Blanc would have been honoured for the rest of his life as the Alpha of his community, pointed out in awed whispers: the war hero who, when everyone else was immobilized by fear, stepped forward and killed the bad man! As it was, he has mostly been regarded as a quixotic hero, a problematic hero, but a hero all the same.

---

* "Introduction" in *Grettir's Saga*, trans. Denton Fox and Hermann Pálsson (University of Toronto Press, 1974), pp. ix–xi. Quoted with the permission of the publisher.

The Beatle Bandit understandably enjoys no such status. And yet … a friend of mine, impeccably law-abiding, always regretted not witnessing the great duel. Seven years old at the time, he was having his hair cut at the plaza and left an hour too early. Many years later he said, a little shamefacedly: "Say what you like, it takes tremendous guts to walk into a bank, jump on the counter, and demand all the money."

♦ ♦ ♦

Along with the pleasures of discovery is the pleasure of meeting and speaking with people who were willing to share their memories, wisdom, and expertise. Many are still alive, while others have passed on since I began my inquiries. They include Rhoda Amiotte, L. John Applegath, Annie Bashutsky, Mary Baxter, Colin and Valerie Beales, Stanley Blanc, Norina D'Agostini, D. Michael Fitz-James, Gerry Goodwin, Edward L. Greenspan QC, Robert Greig, Marilyn Gurney, Todd Hillhouse, Richard Himel, Gordon Hobson, Margaret Burns Hogan, Ron Kasman, Sue Laidlaw, Carman Lamb, W. Herbert Langdon QC, Derek Lundy, Lonna Mackie, Kirk Makin, Dr. Robert J. McCaldon, Paul McIlroy, Peter McSherry, Robert G. Murray QC, The Hon. Justice John G.J. O'Driscoll, Wayne Oldham, Harvey O'Neil, The Hon. Justice William D. Parker, Alvin Pollock, Jindra Rutherford, John Sampson QC, Dr. Miriam Anne Skey, Dr. Ronald E. Stokes, Margaret Timmins, and Joan M. Wales.

My late and beloved wife, Heather McArthur, was an unfailing source of insight and encouragement. And I can hardly overstate the kindness and graciousness shown to her and me by Eileen Griffiths MacDonald and her children — Estelle Griffiths, Kerry Matthew Griffiths (and his wife Cindy), Wagner and Ryan MacDonald, and by Lianne and Dr. Robert Forward, Coleen Forward, and Robin Forward, and the other members of the family we were privileged to meet.

To all of them, and any others I have inadvertently left out, I will always be deeply grateful.

—Paul Truster

Paul Truster is a retired legal educator and sometime freelance writer based in Toronto.

Acknowledgements

I wish to thank Paul Truster, who first alerted me to the fascinating story of the Beatle Bandit and provided copious research material and editorial advice. This book would not have been possible without Paul's input.

I also wish to thank Scott Fraser at Dundurn Press for his interest in this book and Dundurn Press for its support and encouragement. I also wish to thank my girlfriend, Jeanne, for her support, love, and research efforts on my behalf, and my parents for supporting, loving, and encouraging me.

I would also like to give a big thanks to Stanley Blanc and Estelle, Kerry, and Cindy Griffiths, for being willing to share details and insights about their respective families.

Bibliography

♦ BOOKS ♦

Barrie, Ron, and Ken Macpherson. *The Ships of Canada's Naval Forces 1910–2002*. St. Catharines, ON: Vanwell Publishing, 2002.

Bercuson, David. *The Secret Army*. Toronto: Lester & Orpen Dennys, 1984.

Brown, Blake. *Arming and Disarming: A History of Gun Control in Canada*. Toronto: University of Toronto Press, 2012.

Canada Year Book 1963–1964. Ottawa: Queen's Printer and Controller of Stationery, 1964.

Canada Year Book 1967. Ottawa: Queen's Printer and Controller of Stationery, 1967.

Canada Year Book 1968. Ottawa: Queen's Printer and Controller of Stationery, 1968.

Cashner, Bob. *The FN FAL Battle Rifle*. Oxford, UK: Osprey Publishing, 2013.

Hoshowsky, Robert. *The Last to Die*. Toronto: Dundurn Press, 2007.

Kendall, Brian. *Our Hearts Went Boom: The Beatles' Invasion of Canada*. Toronto: Penguin Books Canada, 1997.

Leyton-Brown, Ken. *The Practice of Execution in Canada*. Vancouver: UBC Press, 2010.

1961 — Census of Canada. Ottawa: Dominion Bureau of Statistics, 1962–1963.

O'Driscoll, John. "Divorce, Abortion and Birth Control." In *Brief to the Bishops: Canadian Catholic Laymen Speak Their Minds*, edited by Paul Harris, 30–40. Don Mills, ON: Longmans Canada, 1965.

Sher, Julian. *Until You Are Dead.* Toronto: Vintage Canada, 2001.

Shorter, Edward, ed. *TPH: History and Memories of the Toronto Psychiatric Hospital, 1925–1966.* Toronto: Wall & Emerson, 1996.

♦ COURT DECISIONS, REPORTS, AND TESTIMONY ♦

Ontario Court of Appeal. *Regina v Matthew Kerry Smith.* September 7, 1965.

Supreme Court of Canada. *In the Supreme Court of Canada — On Appeal From the Court of Appeal for Ontario.* November 17, 1965.

Supreme Court of Canada. *In the Supreme Court of Canada — On Appeal From the Court of Appeal for Ontario.* Affidavit by Dr. Arthur Blair. November 17, 1965.

Supreme Court of Canada. *In the Supreme Court of Canada — On Appeal From the Court of Appeal for Ontario.* Affidavit by Dr. Gary Cormack. November 17, 1965.

Supreme Court of Ontario. *In the Matter of the Matrimonial Causes Act Between Warren John Laidlaw and Diane Judith Laidlaw.* June 23, 1967.

Supreme Court of Ontario. *Regina v Matthew Kerry Smith.* Denison Armoury Robbery December 8, 1963, summary. Detective Edward Blakeley, Detective Forbes Ewing. Undated.

Supreme Court of Ontario. *Regina v Matthew Kerry Smith.* Imperial Bank of Canada Robbery February 9, 1960, summary. Detective Forbes Ewing. Undated.

Supreme Court of Ontario. *Regina v Matthew Kerry Smith.* Reports and Statements by Detective Forbes Ewing, Police Constable Robert Greig, Detective Sergeant Norman Hobson, Police Constable Klaus Hubner, Police Constable Donald Jackson, Police Constable Edward Jessop, Deputy Crown Attorney Herbert Langdon, Dr. Chester McLean, John O'Driscoll, Justice William D. Parker, Detective James Read, Police Constable William Roberts, Detective Sergeant David Saunders, Detective George Thompson, Detective Sergeant John Webster, Sergeant of Detectives David Williamson. May 1965.

Supreme Court of Ontario. *Regina v Matthew Kerry Smith.* Testimony of Andrea Ackarman, Detective Brian Albright, Kenneth Amiotte, Joseph Bashutzky, Sally Blanc, Harry Louis Caesar, Duncan Carolan, Jack Cherlon, Detective Gordon Clydesdale, Detective

Harold Coon, Detective Robert Dougall, Dr. Norman Easton, Police
Sergeant Ernest Gibson, Detective Ralph Gilbert, Police Constable
Robert Greig, Eileen Charity Griffiths, Detective Sergeant Norman
Hobson, Joan Hoffman, Police Constable Klaus Hubner, Dr. Harry
Hutchison, Dr. Herbert Hyland, Detective Sergeant Maurice Inglis,
Police Constable Donald Jackson, Detective John Jamieson, Police
Constable Edward Jessop, Vaclav Krcma, Carman Lamb, Robert
Lawrence, Hartley Lepofsky, Detective Sergeant Roderick Marsh,
Henry Martens, Dr. Chester McLean, Detective James Read, Richard
Skey, Dr. Ronald Stokes, Dr. Michael Tuchtie, Detective Sergeant
John Webster, Stanley Willison. Toronto, Ontario, May 10–19, 1965.

Supreme Court of Ontario. *Regina v Matthew Kerry Smith.* Toronto
Dominion Bank Robbery December 24, 1963, summary, Detective
Edward Blakeley, Detective Forbes Ewing. Undated.

Supreme Court of Ontario. *Writ Issued the 7th Day of May 1952 Between
Matthew Smith (Plaintiff) and Helen Isabel Smith and Joseph Drury
(Defendants).*

♦ DIRECTORIES ♦

Might's 1960 Greater Toronto City Directory. Toronto: Might Directories
Limited, 1960.

Might's 1964 Greater Toronto City Directory. Toronto: Might Directories
Limited, 1964.

Might's 1965 Greater Toronto City Directory. Toronto: Might Directories
Limited, 1965.

1954 Toronto City Directory. Toronto: Might Directories Limited, 1954.

♦ DOCUMENTS ♦

Canada, Governor General in Council. Commutation of Matthew Kerry
Smith's Sentence, November 29, 1965.

Canada, House of Commons. "Commutations of Death Sentences."
Debates, 26th Parliament, 3rd Session, vol. 3. June 14, 1965.

Canadian Friends Service Committee. "Letter to Prime Minister Lester B.
Pearson." November 21, 1965.

Department of Justice, Canada. *Capital Punishment: Material Relating to
Its Purpose and Value.* Ottawa: Queen's Printer, 1965.

Department of Justice, Canada. "Memorandum." September 13, 1965.

Dominion of Canada. *Certificate of Naturalization, Smith family.* March
10, 1920.

Government of Canada, Minister of Justice. "Regulations Prescribing
    Certain Firearms and Other Weapons, Components and Parts of
    Weapons, Accessories, Cartridge Magazines, Ammunition and
    Projectiles as Prohibited, Restricted (SOR/98-462)." Last amended
    May 1, 2020. laws-lois.justice.gc.ca/eng/regulations/sor-98-462/index.
    html.

Government of Canada, Order in Council. "Prohibited Weapons Order,
    No. 13." November 29, 1994 (published December 14, 1994, in
    Canada Gazette Part II, 128, no. 25).

Government of Canada, Order in Council. "Restricted Weapons Order,
    Amendment." December 23, 1982 (published January 12, 1983 in
    Canada Gazette Part II, 117, no. 1).

Government of Canada. *Prefix to Statutes, 1953–1954: Acts Proclaimed
    in Force.* "An Act Respecting the Criminal Law (Criminal Code),"
    Assented to June 26, 1954. Ottawa: Queen's Printer, 1954.

House of Commons, Canada. *Bill 391 — An Act to Amend the Criminal
    Code.* First Reading, June 19, 1951.

Juristat, Canadian Centre for Justice Statistics. "Homicides by Province/
    Territory." Table 2, page 4, in Mia Dauvergne, *Homicide in Canada,
    2001.* Statistics Canada catalogue no. 85-002-XIE 22, no. 7. Ottawa:
    Statistics Canada.

Kaufman, Fred. *In the Matter of an Application by Steven Murray Truscott
    Pursuant to Section 690 (Now 696.1) of the Criminal Code.* "Executive
    Summary." Ottawa: Government of Canada, Department of Justice.
    April 19, 2004.

Metropolitan Toronto Police. *Auto List #9.* February 28, 1965.

Metropolitan Toronto Police. "Murder and Bank Robbery Reward
    $7,000." Circular, July 25, 1964.

Metropolitan Toronto Police. "Statement of Matthew Kerry Smith,
    January 7, 1965."

Nowlan, George, Progressive Conservative (Digby-Annapolis — Kings,
    Nova Scotia). Contribution to House of Commons debate on
    "Various Amendments Relating to Offensive Weapons, Penalty
    for Offences of a Seditious Nature, Improper Use of Mails, Etc."
    House of Commons Debates, 21st Parliament, 4th Session: vol. 5.
    June 25, 1951. Image 638, page 4656. parl.canadiana.ca/view/oop.
    debates_HOC2104_05/638?r=0&s=4.

Parker, William. "Report of the Honorable Mr. Justice W.D. Parker Upon
    the Capital Case of Regina Versus Matthew Kerry Smith." Submitted
    to Minister of Justice Guy Favreau, May 26, 1965.

Parliament of the Dominion of Canada. *Public General Acts*, vol. 1, *The Criminal Code*. 1892.

Province of Manitoba. Official Notice of Birth, Eileen Charity Amiotte. Signed February 7, 1944.

Smith, Matt. "Chore List." Signed by Matthew Kerry Smith, March 11, 1952.

Solicitor General of Canada. *Capital Punishment: New Material: 1965– 1972*. Ottawa: Information Canada, 1972.

Statistics Canada, Judicial Division. "Ten Year Firearm Study, 1961–1974," revised February 1976.

Vrandenburg, Bill. "Canadian River Class Frigates." Fact Sheet No. 21. Ottawa: Friends of the Canadian War Museum, n.d.

♦ **INTERVIEWS** ♦

Blanc, Stanley. By author. Skype, February 7 and 9, 2021.

Greenspan, Stanley. By author. Phone, June 24, 2020.

Griffiths, Cindy. By author. Emails, January 12, 2021, Zoom, December 2, 2020.

Griffiths, Estelle. By author. Phone, August 30, 2020.

Griffiths, Kerry. By author. Zoom, December 2, 2020.

Lamb, Carman. By author. Phone, July 2, 2020.

Lesk, Stan. By author. Skype, June 24, 2020.

♦ **LETTERS (IN THE AUTHOR'S POSSESSION, USED WITH PERMISSION OF FAMILY)** ♦

Eileen Charity Griffiths to Matthew Bartley Smith and Anne Bartley Smith, April 6, 1976.

Helen Isabel Smith to Matthew Kerry Smith, January 20, 1958.

Matthew Bartley Smith to Matthew Kerry Smith, January 28, 1958.

Matthew Bartley Smith to Matthew Kerry Smith, February 10, 1958.

Matthew Bartley Smith to Matthew Kerry Smith, February 16, 1958.

Matthew Bartley Smith to Matthew Kerry Smith, undated.

Matthew Bartley Smith to Monny, November 8, 1952.

Matthew Bartley Smith to Monny and Ab, February 9, 1942.

Matthew Bartley Smith to Monny and Ab, March 5, 1942.

Matthew Bartley Smith to Monny and Ab, August 18, 1951.

Matthew Kerry Smith to Eileen Charity Amiotte, August 11, 1965.

Matthew Kerry Smith to Eileen Charity Amiotte, September 1, 1965.

Matthew Kerry Smith to Eileen Charity Amiotte, postmarked October 6, 1965.

Matthew Kerry Smith to Eileen Charity Amiotte, November 9, 1965.

Matthew Kerry Smith to Eileen Charity Amiotte, January 22, 1966.

Matthew Kerry Smith to Eileen Charity Amiotte, February 14, 1966.

Matthew Kerry Smith to Eileen Charity Amiotte, Postmarked March 30, 1966.

♦ PERIODICALS ♦

Adams, Frank. "Commutation of Death Sentences Assailed." *Globe and Mail*, September 15, 1965.

Adler, Mike. "Bathurst Manor Plaza to be Torn Down After Decades as a Community Fixture." *North York Mirror*, July 26, 2016.

Anderson, Alan. "He Knew He Robbed With a Killer." *Toronto Telegram*, June 29, 1965.

Blue Line Magazine. "Metropolitan Toronto Police Milestones." November 2007.

Canadian Jewish News. "Drive Launched for Support of Hero's Family." July 31, 1964.

Carmichael, David. "Bank Customer Killed in Bid to Halt Bandit." *Globe and Mail*, July 25, 1964.

Cederburg, Fred. "Beatle Bandit's Suicide Almost Inevitable, Jury Told." *Toronto Telegram*, July 14, 1966.

Collister, Ron. "'As Free as the Vote on the Flag.'" *Daily Colonist*, December 11, 1965.

———. "A Not-So-Free Vote on Hanging." *The Brandon Sun*, December 8, 1965.

Feeny, Edwin. "'Give Up, Arthur,' His Mother Pleads as She Reads Bible." *Toronto Daily Star*, May 21, 1955.

Ferenc, Leslie. "Son Fights To Preserve Mother's Land." *Toronto Star*, December 23, 1998.

Gibb, Alexandrine, and Frank Teskey. "I Didn't Shoot My Gun, I Was Sucker — Simpson Says Whiskey to Blame." *Toronto Daily Star*, May 20, 1955.

Globe and Mail. "Accused as Beatle-Wig Slayer, Pleads Worsening Schizophrenia." May 18, 1965.

———. "Accused as Murder Accessory, Man Says He Disposed of Wig." February 12, 1965.

————. "Armed and Very Dangerous, Second Bank Bandit Sought." May 20, 1955.

————. "Aronson Is Captured; Flight West Foiled." May 30, 1955.

————. "Arsenal Seized; Man, 24, Charged in Beatle Killing." January 8, 1965.

————. "Bank Bandit Shoots Teller in Don Mills." February 10, 1960.

————. "Baptists Seek Commutation in Bank Killing." September 24, 1965.

————. "Beatle Bandit's Friend Admits Beating Officer, Robbing Bank." June 26, 1965.

————. "'Beatle' Trial Witnesses Clash on How Blanc Got Gun." May 11, 1965.

————. "Beatle-Wig Suspect Admirer of Violent Men, Witness Says." May 13, 1965.

————. "'Blanc Bravest Man I Fought': Statement Read in Death Trial." May 14, 1965.

————. "Bought Brampton Apartments with Bank-Raid Haul: Witness." May 15, 1965.

————. "Boy Born on Same Day as Nation." April 21, 1961.

————. "Cabinet to Deal with Sentence of Beatle Bandit." November 27, 1965.

————. "Chief to Protest Life Sentence Given Bandit." December 2, 1965.

————. "Condemned to Hang, Father of Baby Boy." July 9, 1965.

————. "Coroner Orders Inquest in Beatle Bandit's Death." June 14, 1966.

————. "Coroner's Jury Urges Bankers Be Instructed to Handle Firearms." November 10, 1955.

————. "Denies Report Bandit Given Execution Stay." September 13, 1965.

————. "Due to Hang, Still Believes in Violence." May 20, 1965.

————. "Four Freed in Blanc Case." May 22, 1965.

————. "A Grisly Tool." December 2, 1965.

————. "Hanging Date for Bank Bandit is Postponed." September 16, 1965.

————. "Jury Decides Today in Slaying of Blanc." May 19, 1965.

————. "Killer's Partner Gets Five Years in Bank Robbery." June 29, 1965.

————. "Lawyers File Appeal to Halt Smith Hanging." September 21, 1965.

————. "Legal Technicality Delays Beatle Bandit's Hanging." September 11, 1965.

————. "Man Held for Trial in Murder at Bank." February 13, 1965.

————. "Metro Detective Gets FBI Course." March 11, 1960.

————. "Murder Ruling Upheld in Beatle Bandit Case." November 18, 1965.

————. "Murder Victim Used to Nab Heroin Seller." May 4, 1962.

————. "Pop Star Faces 2 Drug Charges." December 9, 1969.

————. "Raiders Shoot 2 in Holdup." November 28, 1964.

————. "Raids Armory, Fails in Try for Sten Guns." December 9, 1963.

————. "Sentence of Death Is Upheld." September 8, 1965.

————. "Smith Family Orders Appeal on Hanging." September 20, 1965.

————. "Suspect Is Remanded in Slaying of Blanc." January 9, 1965.

————. "Toronto Records (weather)." January 7, 1965.

————. "Toronto Records (weather)." January 9, 1965.

————. "Tribute Paid to Blanc; Police Pressing Hunt for Beatle Bandit." July 27, 1964.

————. "Witness Describes Gun Battle, Shot by Shot." May 12, 1965.

————. "Would You Hang This Man?" September 11, 1965.

Glynn, Douglas. "Chance Creates a Killer." *Globe and Mail*, August 8, 1964.

————. "Check One Car Off Wanted List." *Globe and Mail*, January 8, 1965.

Griffiths, Phyllis. "I'll Try to Stick by Him Mother-to-Be Says of Suspect." *Toronto Telegram*, January 9, 1965.

Hanlon, Michael. "Norman Hobson, Top Detective." *Toronto Star*, August 5, 1998.

Hawes, John, and Norman McCaud. "For the Sake of Argument: We're Denying Prisoners the Right to Learn." *Maclean's*, November 1967.

Heaps, Leo. "Toronto Bank Robber Killed Israel Combat Veteran." *Canadian Jewish News*, April 11, 1985.

Johnstone, Robert. "Modern-Day Police Are Crime Scientists." *Toronto Daily Star*, June 15, 1965.

Lake Simcoe Advocate. "Two Shot During Friday Bank Robbery." December 3, 1964.

Leblanc, Dave. "Bathurst Manor's Mid-Century Modern Homes Have

Survived on the Modesty of Their Owners." *Globe and Mail*, July 6, 2017.

Lungen, Paul. "Bathurst Manor Plaza to Close Forever on July 31." *Canadian Jewish News*, June 21, 2016.

Makin, Kirk. "Judge Made 'Flagrant' Errors, Appeal Court Says." *Globe and Mail*, February 2, 2007.

———. "Judging the Judges." *Globe and Mail*, February 26, 2005.

Mays, John Bentley. "Suburbia's Not Boring If You're Escaping Persecution." *Globe and Mail*, July 2, 1997.

Montreal Gazette. "Chief Scores Commutation." December 2, 1965.

Newmarket Era and Express. "Two Bandits Raid Sutton Bank Friday." December 2, 1964.

Porter, McKenzie. "The 6-Gun Reign is Over." *Toronto Telegram*, July 28, 1964.

Powell, Betsy. "From 12 Years Old to 95: Toronto's Victims of Homicide in Another Year Dominated by Gun Violence." *Toronto Star*, December 31, 2020.

Ross, Alexander. "The Menace of Insane Killers at Large," *Maclean's*, February 5, 1966.

Saskatoon Star Phoenix. Eileen MacDonald obituary. July 28, 2010.

Smith, Matt Bartley. "How to Crash and Live." *Magazine Digest*, November 1944.

———. "Teeter-Totter for the Drowned." *Magazine Digest*, August 1944.

Stuebing, Ted. "Sniping At Our Gun Law: It's a Wavering Target." *Toronto Telegram*, July 28, 1964.

———. "Thug Apologizes After Wounding 2 Bank Employees." *Toronto Telegram*, November 28, 1964.

———. "$2,000 Reward for Killer." *Toronto Telegram*, July 25, 1964.

Toronto Daily Star. "Abducted Girl Safe As Police Trap Bank Suspects." July 24, 1964.

———. "Bandit Shoots Teller." February 9, 1960.

———. "Barrage of Beefs Hits City Hall." July 24, 1964.

———. "Barry, Johnson to Meet on Civil Rights." July 24, 1964.

———. "'Beatle' Bandit Loses Appeal — to Hang Sept. 22." September 8, 1965.

———. "'Beatle' Bandit One of 3 Saved From Gallows." December 1, 1965.

———. "'Beatle' Bank Bandit Shoots Customer Dead." July 25, 1964.

———. "Beatle Wig Bandit Slashes Wrists, Dies." June 13, 1966.

———. "Detective Passes FBI Course." June 9, 1960.

———. Entertainment Listings. July 24, 1964.

———. "Girl, Guns, Bullet-Riddled Door Found in Lightning Raid." January 8, 1965.

———. "Grab Arsenal, Arrest 4 in Beatle-Wig Slaying." January 8, 1965.

———. "'I Wish It Was Me Who Was Shot Dead.'" May 20, 1955.

———. "Insanity Defense of Man Charged in Blanc Killing." May 18, 1965.

———. "Jews Honour Jack Blanc Killed Tackling Gunman." October 4, 1965.

———. "Kingston 'Archaic Dungeon,' Crown Tells Beatle Inquest." July 14, 1966.

———. "Launch Telephone Blitz for John Blanc Fund." August 4, 1964.

———. "Man Charged in Bank Killing." January 7, 1965.

———. "Man Committed in Bank Slaying." February 13, 1965.

———. "'Merry Christmas' From Bank Robber." December 26, 1963.

———. "Metro Armory Bandit Foiled." December 9, 1963.

———. "'Might Get Life, Couldn't Take It, Wish My Gun Had Killed Teller.'" May 30, 1955.

———. "No Hangings on the Eve of Vote." December 3, 1965.

———. "Reward $7,000 for Beatle-Wig Bandit." July 27, 1964.

———. "'Shooting At All Hours,' Says Murder-Suspect's Neighbor." January 8, 1965.

———. "Shot Dead — Toronto Bandits Kill Man in Bank." May 19, 1955.

———. "Simpson Given Twenty Years Aronson Committed for Trial." June 30, 1955.

———. "Stole Car Because His Stolen." February 11, 1961.

———. "Tell-Tale Licence, Clicked in His Mind." January 8, 1965.

Toronto Telegram. "Beatle Bandit's Sanity Still Queried." June 14, 1966.

———. "The Eagle-Eyed Officer." January 8, 1965.

———. "Fiancee Prays While Teller Fights for Life." February 10, 1960.

———. "5 In Court Under Heavy Guard." January 8, 1965.

———. "Full Military Honors Mark Burial of Slain Veteran." July 27, 1964.

———. "Gunfire in Bank Holdup." May 21, 1955.

———. "Gunman Tied Two at Armories, Sought Sten Guns." December 9, 1963.

———. "Gunman Warned His Victim — Police." May 13, 1965.

———. "He Ignored His Wife's Pleas." July 25, 1964.

———. "Hero's Welcome for PC Who Nabbed Murder Suspect." January 8, 1965.

———. "I Tried to Stop Husband Chasing Bandit — Widow." May 10, 1965.

———. "'Kill or Be Killed,' Pal Quotes Accused." May 14, 1965.

———. "Loyalty and Fear Forced Silence, Murder Case Told." May 15, 1965.

———. "Masked Man Joked as Money Placed in Bag." May 11, 1965.

———. "Murder Trial Without Jury." May 12, 1965.

———. "Robs Banker After Teller Shot in Head." February 9, 1960.

———. "'Thought It Was a Joke'." July 25, 1964.

———. "'Throw the Book at Me' Thief Laughs." February 10, 1961.

———. "The Tip That Led to the Jack Blanc Arrests." January 8, 1965.

———. "Trio Held in Holdup Slaying." January 7, 1965.

———. "2-Gun Man Withdraws $12,000." December 26, 1963.

———. "Weapons: Let's Control Them." July 29, 1964.

———. "Woman, 4 Men Are Held." January 8, 1965.

Wales, Joan (as told to Jindra Rutherford). "The Beatle Bandit Bought Their Car." *Toronto Daily Star,* May 19, 1966.

Walker, John. "3 Death Sentences Commuted by Gov't." *Winnipeg Tribune,* December 1, 1965.

Westell, Anthony. "Three Murderers Given Reprieve." *Globe and Mail,* December 1, 1965.

Winnipeg Tribune. "Chief Protests Sparing of Killer." December 2, 1965.

Young, Scott. "The Beatle Bandit Appeal." *Globe and Mail,* September 20, 1965.

———. "A Father Talks About His Son, the Murderer.' *Globe and Mail,* September 10, 1965.

———. "Jury Rules Beatle Bandit's Death a Suicide, Finds No Neglect by Prison." *Globe and Mail,* July 14, 1966.

———. "Postscript to a Suicide." *Globe and Mail,* June 24, 1966.

———. "The Razor Blade." *Globe and Mail,* June 15, 1966.

———. "Thoughts Before the Hanging." *Globe and Mail,* September 16, 1965.

♦ RADIO ♦

CHUM Hit Parade, Toronto, Week of July 20, 1964.

CHUM Hit Parade, Toronto, Week of March 23, 1964.

♦ TELEVISION ♦

Toronto File. "The Case of the Beatle Bandit." Aired November 29, 1965, on CBLT.

———. "The Vigilante." Aired September 28, 1964, on CBC Television.

♦ WEBSITES ♦

Bothwell, Robert. "Lester B. Pearson." In *The Canadian Encyclopedia.* Published online July 6, 2011, last edited February 10, 2021. tinyurl. com/sxpj6sw.

Canada's Historic Places. "Old Toronto City Hall and York County Court House National Historic Site of Canada." tinyurl.com/4sau67p7.

CBC Learning. "The October Crisis." In "Years of Hope and Anger: 1964–1976," episode 16 of *Canada: A People's History.* Broadcast January 12, 2002. tinyurl.com/2cfecyrj.

City of Toronto. "Bathurst Manor," Hood #34 in *Neighbourhood Profiles.* Toronto, n.d. toronto.ca/city-government/data-research-maps/neighbourhoods-communities/neighbourhood-profiles/.

———. "Toronto at a Glance." tinyurl.com/3p7fsc52.

Conroy, Ed. "That Time When CKEY590 Was Toronto AM Gold." *Blogto,* October 11, 2013. blogto.com/city/2013/10/that_time_when_ckey590_was_toronto_am_gold/.

Correctional Service Canada. "Abolition of the Death Penalty 1976." In *50 Years of Human Rights Developments in Federal Corrections.* Ottawa: Government of Canada, 2015. csc-scc.gc.ca/text/pblct/rht-drt/index-eng.shtml.

———. "History of the Canadian Correctional System." A module in the Canadian History course. csc-scc.gc.ca/educational-resources/092/ha-student-etudiant-eng.pdf.

Find a Grave. "Eileen Charity Amiotte MacDonald." findagrave.com/memorial/208608769/eileen-charity-macdonald/photo.

———. "Lianne Belle Smith Forward." findagrave.com/memorial/202592004/lianne-belle-forward.

Gendreau, Paul, and Wayne Renke. "Capital Punishment in Canada." In *The Canadian Encyclopedia.* Published online February 6, 2006, last edited November 6, 2020. tinyurl.com/enk64xmv.

Google Maps. "221 Wilmington Avenue, Toronto." tinyurl.com/5kcb9f5s.

———. "Bathurst Manor." tinyurl.com/fpz348w.

———. "Sutton, Ontario." tinyurl.com/9v6ju8n7.

———. "Yonge Street and Castlefield Avenue."
tinyurl.com/bhhn9db4.

Government of Canada. "HMCS *Cornwallis*/Shore Establishment."
In *Royal Canadian Navy History, Ships' Histories*. Last modified 21
October, 2020. tinyurl.com/2dz8zac7.

Keeseekoowenin Ojibway First Nation. keeseekoowenin.ca.

Lake Simcoe Region Conservation Authority. "Lake Simcoe Watershed."
lsrca.on.ca/our-watershed.

Listing|ca. "2900 Yonge Street." toronto.listing.ca/2900/yonge-st.htm.

McIntosh, Andrew, updater. "The Great Flag Debate." In *The Canadian
Encyclopedia*. Published online February 7, 2006, last edited
December 11, 2019. thecanadianencyclopedia.ca/en/article/
flag-debate.

"The M'Naghten Rule," FindLaw, tinyurl.com/bnezh268.

Mustapha [pseud.]. "Miscellany Toronto Photographs: Then and Now."
Urban Toronto, December 5, 2011. urbantoronto.ca/forum/threads/
miscellany-toronto-photographs-then-and-now.6947/page-483.

Neighbourhood Guide. "Willowdale." tinyurl.com/34nubxmn.

"1963–1964 Toronto Maple Leafs," NHL, tinyurl.com/2kpvf33k.

The Old Farmer's Almanac. "Weather History for Toronto, ON — January
6, 1965." tinyurl.com/86mubfwa.

———. "Weather History for Toronto, ON — January 8, 1965."
tinyurl.com/p5w8a49a.

———. "Weather History for Toronto, ON — July 24, 1964." tinyurl
.com/y5hm4rnd.

Parliament of Canada. "Philip Gerald Givens." lop.parl.ca/sites/ParlInfo/
default/en_CA/People/Profile?personId=5473.

———. "The Right Honourable Lester Bowles Pearson" ourcommons
.ca/About/HistoryArtsArchitecture/fine_arts/prime_ministers/645-e
.htm.

Pickering College. "Welcome." In *About Pickering College*. pickeringcollege
.on.ca/about.

Proctor Funeral Home. "Lianne Belle Forward." Camden, AR:
Proctor Funeral Home, 2019. proctorfuneralhome.com/obituary/
lianne-forward.

Royal Canadian Mounted Police. "History of Firearms in Canada." Last
modified April 22, 2020. Ottawa: Government of Canada.
tinyurl.com/bck7yxak.

Statistics Canada. "Census Profile, 2016 Census: Rolling River 67B,

Indian Reserve [Census subdivision], Manitoba and Manitoba [Province]." www12.statcan.gc.ca/census-recensement/2016/dp-pd/prof/details/page.cfm?B1=All&Code1=4615072&Code2=46&Data=Count&Geo1=CSD&Geo2=PR&Lang=E&SearchPR=01&Search-Text=Rolling+River+67B&SearchType=Begins&TABID=1.

———. "Murder, Persons Charged, Acquitted and Convicted, Canada, 1961 to 1975 (Table Z109-113)." Modified June 22, 2021. Ottawa: Government of Canada. Accessible from www150.statcan.gc.ca/n1/pub/11-516-x/sectionz/Z109_113-eng.csv.

Toronto Police Service. "Homicide ASR RC TBL 002." Last updated March 22, 2021, data.torontopolice.on.ca/datasets/5d7eee403ca34d3692475ee4651d0a07_0/explore.

♦ ADDITIONAL SOURCE MATERIAL ♦

"Good Guys Good Citizen Award." CKEY Radio 59. Presented to PC Robert Greig, January 12, 1965.

Image Credits

Index

Page references in italics indicate images.

About the Author

Nate Hendley is a Toronto-based freelance writer. He is the author of several books, primarily in the true-crime genre. His titles include *The Boy on the Bicycle: A Forgotten Case of Wrongful Conviction in Toronto*; *The Big Con: Great Hoaxes, Frauds, Grifts, and Swindles in American History*; and *Steven Truscott: Decades of Injustice*. For more information about Nate's books and background, visit his website at natehendley.com or his crime blog at crimestory.wordpress.com.